LOVE LETTERS

NATHANIEL HAWTHORNE

TO MISS PEABODY

Oak Hill, April 13th, 1841

Ownest love,

Here is thy poor husband in a polar Paradise! I know not how to interpret this aspect of Nature—whether it be of good or evil omen to our enterprise. But I reflect that the Plymouth pilgrims arrived in the midst of storm and stept ashore upon mountain snow-drifts; and nevertheless they prospered, and became a great people—and doubtless it will be the same with us. I laud my stars, however, that thou wilt not have thy first impressions of our future home from such a day as this. Thou wouldst shiver all thy life afterwards, and never realise that there could be bright skies, and green hills and meadows, and trees heavy with foliage, when now the whole scene is a great snow-bank, and the sky full of snow likewise. Through faith, I persist in believing that spring and summer will come in their due season; but the unregenerated man shivers within me, and suggests a 4 doubt whether I may not have wandered within the precincts of the Arctic circle, and chosen my heritage among everlasting snows. Dearest, provide thyself with a good stock of furs; and if thou canst obtain the skin of a polar bear, thou wilt find it a very suitable summer dress for this region. Thou must not hope ever to walk abroad, except upon snow-shoes, nor to find any warmth, save in thy husband's heart.

Belovedest, I have not yet taken my first lesson in agriculture, as thou mayst well suppose—except that I went to see our cows foddered, yesterday afternoon. We have eight of our own; and the number is now increased by a transcendental heifer, belonging to Miss Margaret Fuller. She is very fractious, I believe, and apt to kick over the milk pail. Thou knowest best, whether in these traits of character, she resembles her mistress. Thy husband intends to convert himself into a milk-maid, this evening; but I pray heaven that Mr. Ripley may be moved to assign him the kindliest cow in the herd—otherwise he will perform his duty with fear and trembling.

Ownest wife, I like my brethren in affliction very well; and couldst thou see us sitting round our table, at meal-times, before the great kitchen-fire, thou wouldst call it a cheerful sight. Mrs. 5 Parker is a most comfortable woman to behold; she looks as if her ample person were stuffed full of tenderness—indeed, as if she were all one great, kind heart. Wert thou here, I should ask for nothing more—not even for sunshine and summer weather; for thou wouldst be both, to thy husband. And how is that cough of thine, my belovedest? Hast thou thought of me, in my perils and wanderings? I trust that thou dost muse upon me with hope and joy; not with repining. Think that I am gone before, to prepare a home for my Dove, and will return for her, all in good time.

Thy husband has the best chamber in the house, I believe; and though not quite so good as the apartment I have left, it will do very well. I have hung up thy two pictures; and they give me a glimpse of summer and of thee. The vase I intended to have brought in my arms, but could not very conveniently do it yesterday; so that it still remains at Mrs. Hillards's, together with my carpet. I shall bring them [at] the next opportunity.

Now farewell, for the present, most beloved. I have been writing this in my chamber; but the fire is getting low, and the house is old and cold; so that the warmth of my whole person has retreated 6 to my heart, which burns with love for thee. I must run down to the kitchen or parlor hearth, when thy image shall sit beside me—yea, be pressed to my breast. At bed-time, thou shalt have a few lines more. Now I think of it, dearest, wilt thou give Mrs. Ripley a copy of Grandfather's Chair and Liberty Tree; she wants them for some boys here. I have several copies of Famous Old People.

April 14th. 10 A.M. Sweetest, I did not milk the cows last night, because Mr. Ripley was afraid to trust them to my hands, or me to their horns—I know not which. But this morning, I have done wonders. Before breakfast, I went out to the barn, and began to chop hay for the cattle; and with such "righteous vehemence" (as Mr. Ripley says) did I labor, that in the space of ten minutes, I broke the machine. Then I brought wood and replenished the fires; and finally sat down to breakfast and ate up a huge mound of buckwheat cakes. After breakfast, Mr. Ripley put a four-pronged instrument into my hands, which he gave me to understand was called a pitch-fork; and he and Mr. Farley being armed with similar weapons, we all then commenced a gallant attack upon a heap of manure. This office being concluded, and thy husband having purified himself, 7 he sits down to finish this letter to his most beloved wife. Dearest, I will never consent that thou come within half a mile of me, after such an encounter as that of this morning. Pray Heaven that his letter retain none of the fragrance with which the writer was imbued. As for thy husband himself, he is peculiarly partial to the odor; but that whimsical little nose of thine might chance to quarrel with it.

Belovedest, Miss Fuller's cow hooks the other cows, and has made herself ruler of the herd, and behaves in a very tyrannical manner. Sweetest, I know not when I shall see thee; but I trust it will not be longer than the end of next week. I love thee! I love thee! I wouldst thou wert with me; for then would my labor be joyful—and even now it is not sorrowful. Dearest, I shall make an excellent husbandman. I feel the original Adam reviving within me.

Miss Sophia A. Peabody,
13 West street,
Boston.

TO MISS PEABODY

Oak Hill, April 16th, ½ past 6
A.M. [1841]

Most beloved, I have a few moments to spare before breakfast; and perhaps thou wilt let me spend them in talking to thee. Thy two letters blessed me yesterday, having been brought by some private messenger of Mrs. Ripley's. Very joyful was I to hear from my Dove, and my heart gave a mighty heave and swell. That cough of thine—I do wish it would take its departure, for I cannot bear to think of thy tender little frame being shaken with it all night long.

Dearest, since I last wrote thee, there has been an addition to our community of four gentlemen in sables, who promise to be among our most useful and respectable members. They arrived yesterday, about noon. Mr. Ripley had proposed to them to join us, no longer ago than that very morning. I had some conversation with them in the afternoon, and was glad to hear them express much satisfaction with their new abode, and all 9 the arrangements. They do not appear to be very communicative, however—or perhaps it may be merely an external reserve, like that of thy husband, to shield their delicacy. Several of their prominent characteristics, as well as their black attire, lead me to believe that they are members of the clerical profession; but I have not yet ascertained from their own lips, what has been the nature of their past lives. I trust to have much pleasure in their society, and, sooner or later, that we shall all of us derive great strength from our intercourse with them. I cannot too highly applaud the readiness with which these four gentlemen in black have thrown aside all the fopperies and flummeries, which have their origin in a false state of society. When I last saw them, they looked as heroically regardless of the stains and soils incident to our profession, as thy husband did when he emerged from the gold mine.

Ownest wife, thy husband has milked a cow!!!

Belovedest, the herd have rebelled against the usurpation of Miss Fuller's cow; and whenever they are turned out of the barn, she is compelled to take refuge under our protection. So much did she impede thy husband's labors, by keeping close to him, that he found it necessary to give her two or three gentle pats with a shovel; but still she 10 preferred to trust herself to my tender mercies, rather than venture among the horns of the herd. She is not an amiable cow; but she has a very intelligent face, and seems to be of a reflective cast of character. I doubt not that she will soon perceive the expediency of being on good terms with the rest of the sisterhood. I have not been twenty yards from our house and barn; but I begin to perceive that this is a beautiful place. The scenery is of a mild and placid character, with nothing bold in its character; but I think its beauties will grow upon us, and make us love it the more, the longer we live here. There is a brook, so near the house that we shall [be] able to hear it ripple, in the summer evenings; but, for agricultural purposes, it has been made to flow in a straight and rectangular fashion, which does it infinite damage, as a picturesque object.

Naughtiest, it was a moment or two before I could think whom thou didst mean by Mr. Dismal View. Why, he is one of the best of the brotherhood, so far as cheerfulness goes; for, if he do not laugh himself, he makes the rest of us laugh continually. He is the quaintest and queerest personage thou didst ever see—full of dry jokes, the humor of which is so incorporated with the strange twistifications of his physiognomy, that his sayings 11 ought to be written down, accompanied with illustrations by Cruikshank. Then he keeps quoting innumerable scraps of Latin, and makes classical allusions, while we are turning over the gold mine; and the contrast between the nature of his employment and the character of his thoughts is irresistibly ludicrous.

Sweetest, I have written this epistle in the parlor, while Farmer Ripley, and Farmer Farley, and Farmer Dismal View, are talking about their agricultural concerns, around the fire. So thou wilt not wonder if it is not a classical piece of composition, either in point of thought or expression. I shall have just time before breakfast is ready—the boy has just come to call us now—but still I will tell thee that I love thee infinitely; and that I long for thee unspeakably, but yet with a happy longing. The rest of them have gone into the breakfast room;...

(Portion of letter missing)

Miss Sophia A. Peabody,
13 West street,
Boston.

TO MISS PEABODY

Brook Farm, April 28th, 1841—7 A.M.

Mine ownest, what a beautiful bright morning is this! I do trust that thou hast not suffered so much from the late tremendous weather, as to be unable now to go abroad in the sunshine. I tremble, almost, to think how thy tender frame has been shaken by that continual cough, which cannot but have grown more inveterate throughout these interminable ages of east wind. At times, dearest, it has seemed an absolute necessity for me to see thee and find out for a certain truth whether thou wert well or ill. Even hadst thou been here, thou wouldst have been penetrated to the core with the chill blast. Then how must thou have been afflicted, where it comes directly from the sea.

Belovedest, thy husband was caught by a cold, during his visit to Boston. It has not affected his whole frame, but took entire possession of his head, as being the weakest and most vulnerable 13 part. Never didst thou hear anybody sneeze with such vehemence and frequency; and his poor brain has been in a thick fog—or rather, it seemed as if his head were stuffed with coarse wool. I know not when I have been so pestered before; and sometimes I wanted to wrench off my head, and give it a great kick, like a foot-ball. This annoyance has made me endure the bad weather with even less than ordinary patience; and my faith was so far exhausted, that, when they told me yesterday that the sun was setting clear, I would not even turn my eyes towards the west. But, this morning, I am made all over anew; and have no greater remnant of my cold, than will serve as an excuse for doing no work to-day. Dearest, do not let Mrs. Ripley frighten thee with apocryphal accounts of my indisposition. I have told thee the whole truth. I do believe that she delights to disquiet people with doubts and fears about their closest friends; for, once or twice, she has made thy cough a bugbear to thy husband. Nevertheless, I will not judge too harshly of the good lady, because I like her very well, in many respects.

The family has been dismal and dolorous, throughout the storm. The night before last, William Allen was stung by a wasp, on the eyelid; 14 whereupon, the whole side of his face swelled to an enormous magnitude; so that, at the breakfast table, one half of him looked like a blind giant (the eye being closed) and the other half had such a sorrowful and ludicrous aspect, that thy husband was constrained to laugh, out of sheer pity. The same day, a colony of wasps was discovered in thy husband's chamber, where they had remained throughout the winter, and were now just bestirring themselves, doubtless with the intention of stinging me from head to foot. Thou wilt readily believe, that not one of the accursed crew escaped my righteous vengeance. A similar discovery was made in Mr. Farley's room. In short, we seem to have taken up our abode in a wasps' nest. Thus thou seest, belovedest, that a rural life is not one of unbroken quiet and serenity.

If the middle of the day prove warm and pleasant, thy husband promises himself to take a walk, in every step of which thou shalt be his companion. Oh, how I long for thee to stay with me; in reality, among the hills, and dales, and woods, of our home. I have taken one walk, with Mr. Farley; and I could not have believed that there was such seclusion, at so short a distance from a great 15 city. Many spots seem hardly to have been visited for ages—not since John Eliot preached to the Indians here. If we were to travel a thousand miles, we could not escape the world more completely than we can here.

Sweetest, I long unspeakably to see thee—it is only the thought of thee that draws my spirit out of this solitude. Otherwise, I care nothing for the world nor its affairs. I read no newspapers, and hardly remember who is President; and feel as if I had no more concern with what other people trouble themselves about, than if I dwelt in another planet. But, still, thou drawest me to thee continually; and so I can realise how a departed spirit feels, while looking back from another world to the beloved ones of this. All other interests appear like shadows and trifles; but love is a reality, which makes the spirit still an inhabitant of the world which it has quitted.

Ownest wife, if Mr. Ripley comes into Boston on Sunday, it is my purpose to accompany him. Otherwise, thou mayst look for me some time during the ensuing week. Be happy, dearest; and above all, do shake off that tremendous cough. Take great care of thyself, and never venture out when there is the least breath of east-wind; but 16 spread thy wings in the sunshine, and be joyous as itself.

God bless thee.

Will thy father have the goodness to leave the letter for Colonel Hall at the Post Office?

Miss Sophia A. Peabody,
13 West street,
Boston.

TO MISS PEABODY

Brook Farm, May 4th, 1841. ½
past 1 P.M.

Belovedest, as Mr. Ripley is going to the city this afternoon, I cannot but write a letter to thee, though I have but little time; for the corn field will need me very soon. My cold no longer troubles me; and all this morning, I have been at work under the clear blue sky, on a hill side. Sometimes it almost seemed as if I were at work in the sky itself; though the material in which I wrought was the ore from our gold mine. Nevertheless, there is nothing so unseemly and disagreeable in this sort of toil, as thou wouldst think. It defiles the hands, indeed, but not the soul. This gold ore is a pure and wholesome substance; else our Mother Nature would not devour it so readily, and derive so much nourishment from it, and return such a rich abundance of good grain and roots in requital of it.

The farm is growing very beautiful now—not 18 that we yet see anything of the pease or potatoes, which we have planted; but the grass blushes green on the slopes and hollows. I wrote that word blush almost unconsciously; so we will let it go as an inspired utterance. When I go forth afield, I think of my Dove, and look beneath the stone walls, where the verdure is richest, in hopes that a little company of violets, or some solitary bud, prophetic of the summer, may be there; to which I should award the blissful fate of being treasured for a time in thy bosom; for I doubt not, dearest, that thou wouldst admit any flowers of thy husband's gathering into that sweetest place. But not a wild flower have I yet found. One of the boys gathered some yellow cowslips, last Sunday; but I am well content not to have found them; for they are not precisely what I should like to send my Dove, though they deserve honor and praise, because they come to us when no others will. We have our parlor here dressed in evergreen, as at Christmas. That beautifullest little flower vase of thine stands on Mr. Ripley's study table, at which I am now writing. It contains some daffodils and some willow blossoms. I brought it here, rather than kept it in my chamber, because I never sit there, and it gives me many pleasant emotions to look round and be surprised (for it is often a surprise, though I well know that 19 it is there) by something which is connected with the idea of thee.

Most dear wife, I cannot hope that thou art yet entirely recovered from that terrible influenza; but if thou art not almost well, I know not how thy husband will endure it. And that cough too. It is the only one of thy utterances, so far as I have heard them, which I do not love. Wilt thou not be very well, and very lightsome, at our next meeting. I promise myself to be with thee next Thursday, the day after tomorrow. It is an eternity since we met; and I can nowise account for my enduring this lengthened absence so well. I do not believe that I could suffer it, if I were not engaged in a righteous and heaven-blessed way of life. When I was in the Custom-House, and then at Salem, I was not half so patient; though my love of thee has grown infinitely since then.

We had some tableaux last evening, the principal characters being sustained by Mr. Farley and Miss Ellen Slade. They went off very well. I would like to see a tableaux arranged by my Dove.

Dearest, I fear it is time for thy clod-compelling husband to take the field again. Good bye.

Miss Sophia A. Peabody,
13 West street,
Boston.

TO MISS PEABODY

Very dearest,

I have been too busy to write thee a long letter by this opportunity; for I think this present life of mine gives me an antipathy to pen and ink, even more than my Custom-House experience did. I could not live without the idea of thee, nor without spiritual communion with thee; but, in the midst of toil, or after a hard day's work in the gold mine, my soul obstinately refuses to be poured out on paper. That abominable gold mine! Thank God, we anticipate getting rid of its treasures, in the course of two or three days. Of all hateful places, that is the worst; and I shall never comfort myself for having spent so many days of blessed sunshine there. It is my opinion, dearest, that a man's soul may be buried and perish under a dung-heap or in a furrow of the field, just as well as under a pile of money. Well; that giant, Mr. George Bradford, will probably be here to-day; 21 so there will be no danger of thy husband being under the necessity of laboring more than he likes, hereafter. Meantime, my health is perfect, and my spirits buoyant, even in the gold mine.

And how art thou, belovedest? Two or three centuries have passed since I saw thee; and then thou wast pale and languid. Thou didst comfort me in that little note of thine; but still I cannot help longing to be informed of thy present welfare. Thou art not a prudent little Dove, and wast naughty to come on such a day as thou didst; and it seems to me that Mrs. Ripley does not know how to take care of thee at all. Art thou quite well now?

Dearest wife, I intend to come and see thee either on Thursday or Friday—perhaps my visit may be deferred till Saturday, if the gold mine should hold out so long. I yearn for thee unspeakably. Good bye now; for the breakfast horn has sounded, some time since. God bless thee, ownest.

THY LOVINGEST
HUSBAND.

Miss Sophia A. Peabody,
13 West street,
Boston.

TO MISS PEABODY

Oh, unutterably ownest wife, no pen can write how I have longed for thee, or for any the slightest word from thee; for thy Sunday's letter did not reach me till noon of this very day! Never was such a thirst of the spirit as I have felt. I began to wonder whether my Dove did really exist, or was only a vision; and canst thou imagine what a desolate feeling that was. Oh, I need thee, my wife, every day, and every hour, and every minute, and every minutest particle of forever and forever.

Belovedest, the robe reached me in due season, and on Sabbath day, I put it on; and truly it imparted such a noble and stately aspect to thy husband, that thou couldst not possibly have known him. He did really look tolerably personable! and, moreover, he felt as if thou wert embracing him, all the time that he was wrapt in the folds of this precious robe. Hast thou made it of such 23 immortal stuff as the robes of Bunyan's Pilgrim were made of? else it would grieve my very heart to subject it to the wear and tear of the world.

Belovedest, when dost thou mean to come home? It is a whole eternity since I saw thee. If thou art at home on a Sunday, I must and will spend it with my ownest wife. Oh, how my heart leaps at the thought.

God bless thee, thou belovedest woman-angel! I cannot write a single word more; for I have stolen the time to write this from the labors of the field. I ought to be raking hay, like my brethren, who will have to labor the longer and later, on account of these few moments which I have given to thee. Now that we are in the midst of haying, we return to our toil, after an early supper. I think I never felt so vigorous as now; but, oh, I cannot be well without thee. Farewell,

TO MISS PEABODY

Dearest unutterably, Mrs. Ripley is going to Boston this morning, to Miss Slade's wedding; so I sit down to write a word to thee, not knowing whither to direct it. My heart searches for thee, but wanders about vaguely, and is strangely dissatisfied. Where art thou? I fear that thou didst spend yesterday in the unmitigated east wind of the seacoast. Perhaps thou art shivering, at this moment.

Dearest, I would that I were with thee. It seems as if all evil things had more power over thee, when I am away. Then thou art exposed to noxious winds, and to pestilence, and to death-like weariness; and, moreover, nobody knows how to take care of thee but thy husband. Everybody else thinks it of importance that thou shouldst paint and sculpture; but it would be no trouble to me, if thou shouldst never touch clay or canvas 25 again. It is not what thou dost, but what thou art, that I concern myself about. And if thy mighty works are to be wrought only by the anguish of thy head, and weariness of thy frame, and sinking of thy heart, then do I never desire to see another. And this should be the feeling of all thy friends. Especially ought it to be thine, for thy husband's sake.

Belovedest, I am very well, and not at all weary; for yesterday's rain gave us a holyday; and moreover the labors of the farm are not as pressing as they have been. And—joyful thought!—in a little more than a fortnight, thy husband will be free from his bondage—free to think of his Dove—free to enjoy Nature—free to think and feel! I do think that a greater weight will then be removed from me, than when Christian's burthen fell off at the foot of the cross. Even my Custom-House experience was not such a thraldom and weariness; my mind and heart were freer. Oh, belovedest, labor is the curse of the world, and nobody can meddle with it, without becoming proportionably brutified. Dost thou think it a praiseworthy matter, that I have spent five golden months in providing food for cows and horses? Dearest, it is not so. Thank God, my soul is not utterly buried under a dung-heap. I shall yet retain 26 it, somewhat defiled, to be sure, but not utterly unsusceptible of purification.

Farewell now, truest wife. It is time that this letter were sealed. Love me; for I love thee infinitely, and pray for thee, and rejoice in thee, and am troubled for thee—for I know not where thou art, nor how thou dost.

Miss Sophia A. Peabody,
Care of Mr. Daniel Newhall,
Lynn, Mass.

TO MISS PEABODY

Brook Farm, 18th Aug. 1841.
½ 12 P.M.

Belovedest, Mrs. Ripley met me at the door, as I came home from work, and told me that Mary was at Mrs. Park's, and that I might have an opportunity to send a message to thee. Whether thou hast written I do not know. At all events, Mrs. Ripley has not yet given me the letter; nor have I had a chance to ask her what she has heard about thee; such a number of troublesome and intrusive people are there in this thronged household of ours. Dearest, if thou hast not written, thou art very sick—one or the other is certain. That wretched and foolish woman! Why could not she have put the letter on my table, so that I might have been greeted by it immediately on entering my room? She is not fit to live.

Dearest, I am very well; only somewhat tired with walking half a dozen miles immediately after breakfast, and raking hay ever since. We shall quite finish haying this week; and then there 28 will be no more very hard or constant labor, during the one other week that I shall remain a slave. Most beloved, I received thy Lynn letter on Saturday, and thy Boston letter yesterday. Then thou didst aver that thou wast very well—but thou didst not call thyself magnificent. Why art thou not magnificent? In thy former letter, thou sayest that thou hast not been so well for two months past. Naughtiest wife, hast thou been unwell for two months?

Ownest, since writing the above, I have been to dinner; and still Mrs. Ripley has given no sign of having a letter for me; nor was it possible for me to ask her—nor do I know when I can see her alone, to inquire about thee. Surely thou canst not have let Mary come without a letter. And if thou art sick, why did she come at all? Belovedest, the best way is always to send thy letters by the mail; and then I shall know where to find them.

Aug. 17th—After breakfast.—Dearest, thou didst not write—that seems very evident. I have not, even yet, had an opportunity to ask Mrs. Ripley about thee; for she was gone out last evening; and when she came back, Miss Ripley and another lady were with her. She mentioned, however, that thy sister Mary looked very bright and 29 happy; so I suppose thou couldst not be very intensely and dangerously sick. I might have asked Mrs. Ripley how thou didst, even in the presence of those two women; but I have an inexpressible and unconquerable reluctance to speak of thee to almost anybody. It seems a sin. Well; I do not feel so apprehensive about thy health as I did yesterday; but, sweetest, if thou hadst sent some distinct message, even though not a letter, it would have saved thy husband some disquietude. Now farewell for the present. I do long to see thee, but know not how to get to thee. Dost thou love me at all? It is a great while since thou hast told me so.

Ownest wife, I meant to have finished this letter this afternoon, and to have sent it by William Allen in the morning; but I have just learnt that Mr. Ripley is about to start for Boston; so I conclude suddenly. God bless thee, and make thee magnificent, and keep thee so forever and ever. I love thee. I love thee.

Do not write to me, if thou art not well.

Miss Sophia A. Peabody,
Boston, Mass.

TO MISS PEABODY

Brook Farm, Aug. 22nd, 1841

Most dear wife, it seems a long time since I have written to thee. Dost thou love me at all? I should have been reprehensible in not writing, the last time Mr. and Mrs. Ripley went to town; but I had an indispensable engagement in the bean-field—whither, indeed, I was glad to betake myself, in order to escape a parting scene with poor Mr. Farley. He was quite out of his wits, the night before, and thy husband sat up with him till long past midnight. The farm is pleasanter now that he is gone; for his unappeasable wretchedness threw a gloom over everything. Since I last wrote to thee, we have done haying; and the remainder of my bondage will probably be light. It will be a long time, however, before I shall know how to make a good use of leisure, either as regards enjoyment or literary occupation.

When am I to see thee again? The first of September comes a week from Tuesday next; but 31 I think I shall ante-date the month, and compel it to begin on Sunday. Wilt thou consent? Then, on Saturday afternoon, (for I will pray Mr. Ripley to give me up so much time, for the sake of my past diligence) I will come to thee, dearest wife, and remain in the city till Monday evening. Thence I shall go to Salem, and spend a week there, longer or shorter according to the intensity of the occasion for my presence. I do long to see our mother and sisters; and I should not wonder if they felt some slight desire to see me. I received a letter from Louisa, a week or two since, scolding me most pathetically for my long absence. Indeed, I have been rather naughty in this respect; but I knew that it would be unsatisfactory to them and myself, if I came only for a single day—and that has been the longest space that I could command.

Dearest wife, it is extremely doubtful whether Mr. Ripley will succeed in locating his community on this farm. He can bring Mr. Ellis to no terms; and the more they talk about the matter, the farther they appear to be from a settlement. Thou and I must form other plans for ourselves; for I can see few or no signs that Providence purposes to give us a home here. I am weary, weary, thrice weary of waiting so many ages. Yet what 32 can be done? Whatever may be thy husband's gifts, he has not hitherto shown a single one that may avail to gather gold. I confess that I have strong hopes of good from this arrangement with Munroe; but when I look at the scanty avails of my past literary efforts, I do not feel authorized to expect much from the future. Well; we shall see. Other persons have bought large estates and built splendid mansions with such little books as I mean to write; so perhaps it is not unreasonable to hope that mine may enable me to build a little cottage—or, at least, to buy or hire one. But I am becoming more and more convinced, that we must not lean upon the community. Whatever is to be done, must be done by thy husband's own individual strength. Most beloved, I shall not remain here through the winter, unless with an absolute certainty that there will be a home ready for us in the spring. Otherwise I shall return to Boston,—still, however, considering myself an associate of the community; so that we may take advantage of any more favorable aspect of affairs. Dearest, how much depends on these little books! Methinks, if anything could draw out my whole strength, it should be the motives that now press upon me. Yet, after all, I must keep these considerations out of my mind, because an external 33 purpose always disturbs, instead of assisting me.

Dearest, I have written the above in not so good spirits as sometimes; but now that I have so ungenerously thrown my despondency on thee, my heart begins to throb more lightly. I doubt not that God has great good in store for us; for He would not have given us so much, unless He were preparing to give a great deal more. I love thee! Thou lovest me! What present bliss! What sure and certain hope!

THINE OWNEST
HUSBAND.

Miss Sophia A. Peabody,
13 West-street,
Boston.

TO MISS PEABODY

—————

Salem, Sept. 3^d, 1841—4
o'clock P.M.

Most beloved,—Thou dost not expect a letter from thy husband; and yet, perhaps, thou wilt not be absolutely displeased should one come to thee tomorrow. At all events, I feel moved to write; though the haze and sleepiness, which always settles upon me here, will certainly be perceptible in every line. But what a letter didst thou write to me! Thou lovest like a celestial being, (as truly thou art,) and dost express thy love in heavenly language;—it is like one angel writing to another angel; but alas! the letter has miscarried, and has been delivered to a most unworthy mortal. Now wilt thou exclaim against thy husband's naughtiness! And truly he is very naughty. Well then; the letter was meant for him, and could not possibly belong to any other being, mortal or immortal. I will trust that thy idea of me is truer than my own consciousness of myself. 35

Dearest, I have been out only once, in the day time, since my arrival. How immediately and irrecoverably (if thou didst not keep me out of the abyss) should I relapse into the way of life in which I spent my youth! If it were not for my Dove, this present world would see no more of me forever. The sunshine would never fall on me, no more than on a ghost. Once in a while, people might discern my figure gliding stealthily through the dim evening—that would be all. I should be only a shadow of the night; it is thou that givest me reality, and makest all things real for me. If, in the interval since I quitted this lonely old chamber, I had found no woman (and thou wast the only possible one) to impart reality and significance to life, I should have come back hither ere now, with the feeling that all was a dream and a mockery. Dost thou rejoice that thou hast saved me from such a fate? Yes; it is a miracle worthy even of thee, to have converted a life of shadows into the deepest truth, by thy magic touch.

Belovedest, I have not yet made acquaintance with Miss Polly Metis. Mr. Foote was not in his office when I called there; so that my introduction to the erudite Polly was unavoidably deferred. I went to the Athenaeum this forenoon, and turned over a good many dusty books. When we dwell 36 together, I intend that my Dove shall do all the reading that may be necessary, in the concoction of my various histories; and she shall repeat the substance of her researches to me. Thus will knowledge fall upon me like heavenly dew.

Sweetest, it seems very long already since I saw thee; but thou hast been all the time in my thoughts; so that my being has been continuous. Therefore, in one sense, it does not seem as if we had parted at all. But really I should judge it to be twenty years since I left Brook Farm; and I take this to be one proof that my life there was an unnatural and unsuitable, and therefore an unreal one. It already looks like a dream behind me. The real Me was never an associate of the community; there has been a spectral Appearance there, sounding the horn at day-break, and milking the cows, and hoeing potatoes, and raking hay, toiling and sweating in the sun, and doing me the honor to assume my name. But be thou not deceived, Dove, of my heart. This Spectre was not thy husband. Nevertheless, it is somewhat remarkable that thy husband's hands have, during the past summer, grown very brown and rough; insomuch that many people persist in believing that he, after all, was the aforesaid spectral horn-sounder, cow-milker, potatoe-hoer, and hay-raker. 37 But such people do not know a reality from a shadow.

Enough of nonsense. Belovedest, I know not exactly how soon I shall return to the Farm. Perhaps not sooner than a fortnight from tomorrow; but, in that case. I shall pay thee an intermediate visit of one day. Wilt thou expect me on Friday or Saturday next, from ten to twelve o'clock on each day,—not earlier nor later.

Miss Sophia A. Peabody,
Care of Dr. N. Peabody,
Boston, Mass.

TO MISS PEABODY

Salem, Septr. 9th, 1841—A.M.

Ownest love,

In my last letter, I left it uncertain whether I should come Friday or Saturday, because I deemed it good to allow myself the freedom of choosing the day that should be most vacant from all earthly care and inconvenience, so that thou mightest be sure to meet the whole of me; and, likewise, I desired to have a brightest and sunniest day, because our meetings have so often been in clouds and drizzle. Also, I thought it well that thy expectation of seeing thy husband should be diffused over two days, so that the disappointment might be lessened, if it were impossible for me to come on the very day appointed. But these reasons are of no moment, since thou so earnestly desirest to know the day and hour. Unless the sky fall, belovedest, I will come tomorrow. I know of no obstacle; and if there were a million, it would be no matter. When once we are together, 39 our own world is round about us, and all things else cease to exist.

Belovedest, thy letter of a week from Thursday reached me not till Tuesday! It had got into the hands of the penny-post. Farewell, ownest. I love thee with infinite intensity, and think of thee continually.

Miss Sophia A. Peabody,
Care of Dr. N. Peabody,
Boston, Mass.

TO MISS PEABODY

Salem, Septr. 10th, 1841—
A.M.

Most dear wife, thou canst not imagine how strange it seems to me that thou shouldst ever suffer any bodily harm. I cannot conceive of it—the idea will not take the aspect of reality. Thou art to me a spirit gliding about our familiar paths; and I always feel as if thou wert beyond the reach of mortal accident—nor am I convinced to the contrary even by thy continual gashings of thy dearest fingers and sprainings of thy ancle. I love thee into the next state of existence, and therefore do not realise that thou art here as subject to corporeal harm as is thy husband himself—nay, ten times more so, because thy earthly manifestation is refined almost into spirit.

But, dearest, thy accident did make thy husband's heart flutter very riotously. I wanted to hold thee in mine arms; for I had a foolish notion that thou wouldst be much better—perhaps quite well! I cannot tell thee all I felt; and still I had not the horrible feelings that I should expect, because there was a shadowiness interposed between me and the fact, so that it did not strike my heart, as the beam did thy head. Let me not speak of it any more, lest it become too real.

Sweetest, thou dost please me much by criticising thy husband's stories, and finding fault with them. I do not very well recollect Monsieur de Miroir; but as to Mrs. Bullfrog, I give her up to thy severest reprehension. The story was written as a mere experiment in that style; it did not come from am depth within me—neither my heart nor mind had anything to do with it. I recollect that the Man of Adamant seemed a fine idea to me, when I looked at it prophetically; but I failed in giving shape and substance to the vision which I saw. I don't think it can be very good.

Ownest wife, I cannot believe all these stories about Munroe, because such an abominable rascal never would be sustained and countenanced by respectable men. I take him to be neither better nor worse than the average of his tribe. However, I intend to have all my copy-rights taken out in my own name; and if he cheats me once, I will have nothing more to do with him, but will straightway be cheated by some other publisher—that being, of course, the only alternative.

Dearest, what dost thou think of taking Governor Shirley's young French wife as the subject of one of the cuts. Thou shouldst represent her in the great chair, perhaps with a dressing glass before her, and arrayed in all manner of fantastic finery, and with an outre French air; while the old Governor is leaning fondly over her, and a Puritan counsellor or two are manifesting their disgust, in the background. A negro footman and French waiting maid might be in attendance. Do not think that I expect thee to adopt my foolish fancies about these things. Whatever thou mayst do, it will be better than I can think. In Liberty Tree, thou mightest have a vignette, representing the chair in a very battered, shattered, and forlorn condition, after it had been ejected from Hutchinson's house. This would serve to impress the reader with the woeful vicissitudes of sublunary things. Many other subjects would thy husband suggest, but he is terribly afraid that thou wouldst take one of them, instead of working out thine own inspirations.

Belovedest, I long to see thee. Do be magnificently well by Saturday—yet not on my account, but thine own. Meantime, take care of thy dearest head. Thou art not fit to be trusted away from thy husband's guidance, one moment. 43

Dear little wife, didst thou ever behold such an awful scribble as thy husband writes, since he became a farmer? His chirography always was abominable; but now it is outrageous.

God bless thee, dearest and may His hand be continually outstretched over thy head. Expect me on Saturday afternoon.

THINE OWNEST
HUSBAND.

Miss Sophia A. Peabody,
Care of Dr. N. Peabody,
Boston, Mass.

TO MISS PEABODY

Salem,   September   14th,
1841—A.M.

Ownest beloved, I know not whether thou dost expect a letter from thy husband; but I have a comfortable faith that it will not be altogether unwelcome; so I boldly sit down to scribble. I love thee transcendently; and nothing makes me more sensible of the fact, than that I write thee voluntary letters, without any external necessity. It is as if intense love should make a dumb man speak. (Alas! I hear a knocking at the door, and suspect that some untimely person is about to call me away from my Dove.)

Afternoon.—Dearest, it was even as I suspected. How sad it is, that we cannot be sure of one moment's uninterrupted communication, even when we are talking together in that same old chamber, where I have spent so many quiet years! Well; thou must be content to lose some very sweet outpourings wherewith my heart would probably have covered the first, and perhaps 45 the second page of this sheet. The amount of all would have been, that I am somewhat partial to thee—and thou hast a suspicion of that fact, already.

Belovedest, Master Cheever is a very good subject for a sketch—especially if thou dost portray him in the very act of executing judgment on an evil-doer. The little urchin may be laid across his knee, and his arms and legs (and whole person, indeed) should be flying all abroad, in an agony of nervous excitement and corporeal smart. The Master, on the other hand, must be calm, rigid, without anger or pity, the very personification of that unmitigable law, whereby suffering follows sin. Meantime, the lion's head should have a sort of sly twist of one side of its mouth, and wink of one eye, in order to give the impression, that, after all, the crime and the punishment are neither of them the most serious things in the world. I would draw this sketch myself, if I had but the use of thy magic fingers. Why dost thou—being one and the same person with thy husband—unjustly keep those delicate little instruments (thy fingers, to wit) all to thyself?

Then, dearest, the Acadians will do very well for the second sketch. Wilt thou represent them as just landing on the wharf?—or as presenting 46 themselves before Governor Shirley, seated in the great chair? Another subject (if this do not altogether suit thee) might be old Cotton Mather, venerable in a three cornered hat and other antique attire, walking the streets of Boston, and lifting up his hands to bless the people, while they all revile him. An old dame should be seen flinging or emptying some vials of medicine on his head, from the latticed window of an old-fashioned house; and all around must be tokens of pestilence and mourning—as a coffin borne along, a woman or children weeping on a door-step. Canst thou paint the tolling of the old South bell?

If thou likest not this subject, thou canst take the military council, holden at Boston by the Earl of Loudoun, and other captains and governors—his lordship in the great chair, an old-fashioned military figure, with a star on his breast. Some of Louis XV's commanders will give thee the costume. On the table and scattered about the room must be symbols of warfare, swords, pistols, plumed hats, a drum, trumpet, and rolled up banner, in one heap. It were not amiss that thou introduce the armed figure of an Indian chief, as taking part in the council—or standing apart from the English, erect and stern.

Now for Liberty tree—there is an engraving of 47 that famous vegetable in Snow's History of Boston; but thou wilt draw a better one out of thine own head. If thou dost represent it, I see not what scene can be beneath it, save poor Mr. Oliver taking the oath. Thou must represent him with a bag wig, ruffled sleeves, embroidered coat, and all such ornaments, because he is the representative of aristocracy and artificial system. The people may be as rough and wild as thy sweetest fancy can make them;—nevertheless, there must be one or two grave, puritanical figures in the midst. Such an one might sit in the great chair, and be an emblem of that stern spirit, which brought about the revolution. But thou wilt find this is a hard subject.

But what a dolt is thy husband, thus to obtrude his counsel in the place of thine own inspiration! Belovedest, I want soon to tell thee how I love thee. Thou must not expect me till Saturday afternoon. I yearn infinitely to see thee. Heaven bless thee forever and forever.

Miss Sophia A. Peabody,
Care of Dr. N. Peabody,
Boston, Mass.

TO MISS PEABODY

Brook Farm, Sept. 22[d], 1841—P.M.

Dearest love, here is thy husband again, slowly adapting himself to the life of this queer community, whence he seems to have been absent half a life time—so utterly has he grown apart from the spirit and manners of the place. Thou knowest not how much I wanted thee, to give me a home-feeling in the spot—to keep a feeling of coldness and strangeness from creeping into my heart and making me shiver. Nevertheless, I was most kindly received; and the fields and woods looked very pleasant, in the bright sunshine of the day before yesterday. I had a friendlier disposition towards the farm, now that I am no longer obliged to toil in its stubborn furrows. Yesterday and to-day, however, the weather has been intolerable—cold, chill, sullen, so that it is impossible to be on kindly terms with Mother Nature. Would I were with thee, mine own warmest and truest-hearted wife!

Belovedest, I doubt whether I shall succeed in 49 writing another volume of Grandfather's Library, while I remain at the farm. I have not the sense of perfect seclusion, which has always been essential to my power of producing anything. It is true, nobody intrudes into my room; but still I cannot be quiet. Nothing here is settled—everything is but beginning to arrange itself—and though thy husband would seem to have little to do with aught beside his own thoughts, still he cannot but partake of the ferment around him. My mind will not be abstracted. I must observe, and think, and feel, and content myself with catching glimpses of things which may be wrought out hereafter. Perhaps it will be quite as well that I find myself unable to set seriously about literary occupation for the present. It will be good to have a longer interval between my labor of the body and that of the mind. I shall work to the better purpose, after the beginning of November. Meantime, I shall see these people and their enterprise under a new point of view, and perhaps be able to determine whether thou and I have any call to cast in our lot among them.

Sweetest, our letters have not yet been brought from the Post Office; so that I have known nothing of thee since our parting. Surely we were very happy—and never had I so much peace and 50 joy as in brooding over thine image, as thou wast revealed to me in our last interview. I love thee with all the heart I have—and more. Now farewell, most dear. Mrs. Ripley is to be the bearer of this letter; and I reserve the last page for tomorrow morning. Perhaps I shall have a blessed word from thee, ere then.

Septr. 23^d—Before breakfast.—Sweetest wife, thou hast not written to me. Nevertheless, I do not conclude thee to be sick, but will believe that thou hast been busy in creating Laura Bridgman. What a faithful and attentive husband thou hast! For once he has anticipated thee in writing.

Belovedest, I do wish the weather would put off this sulky mood. Had it not been for the warmth and brightness of Monday, when I arrived here, I should have supposed that all sunshine had left Brook Farm forever. I have no disposition to take long walks, in such a state of the sky; nor have I any buoyancy of spirit. Thy husband is a very dull person, just at this time. I suspect he wants thee. It is his purpose, I believe, either to walk or ride to Boston, about the end of next week, and give thee a kiss—after which he will return quietly and contentedly to the farm. Oh, what joy, when he will again see thee every day! 51

We had some tableaux last night. They were very stupid, (as, indeed, was the case with all I have ever seen) but do not thou tell Mrs. Ripley so. She is a good woman, and I like her better than I did—her husband keeps his old place in my judgment. Farewell, thou gentlest Dove—thou perfectest woman—

THINE OWNEST
HUSBAND.

Miss Sophia A. Peabody,
Boston, Mass.

TO MISS PEABODY

Brook Farm, Septr. 25th, 1841—½ past 7 A.M.

Ownest Dove, it was but just now that I thought of sending thee a few lines by Mr. Ripley; for this penning of epistles is but a wretched resource. What shall I do? What shall I do? To talk to thee in this way does not bring thee nearer; it only compels me to separate myself from thee, and put thee at a distance. Of all humbugs, pretending to alleviate mortal woes, writing is the greatest.

Yet, thy two letters were a great comfort to me—so great, that they could not possibly have been dispensed with. Dearest, I did not write thee what Mr. and Mrs. Ripley said to me, because they have said nothing which I did not know before. The ground, upon which I must judge of the expediency of our abiding here, is not what they may say, but what actually is, or is likely to be; and of this I doubt whether either of them is capable 53 of forming a correct opinion. Would that thou couldst he here—or could have been here all summer— in order to help me think what is to be done. But one thing is certain—I cannot and will not spend the winter here. The time would be absolutely thrown away, so far as regards any literary labor to be performed,—and then to suffer this famished yearning for thee, all winter long! It is impossible.

Dearest, do not thou wear thyself out with working upon that bust. If it cause thee so much as a single head-ache, I shall wish that Laura Bridgman were at Jericho. Even if thou shouldst not feel thyself wearied at the time, I fear that the whole burthen of toil will fall upon thee when all is accomplished. It is no matter if Laura should go home without being sculptured—no matter if she goes to her grave without it. I dread to have thee feel an outward necessity for such a task; for this intrusion of an outward necessity into labors of the imagination and intellect is, to me, very painful.

Oh, what weather! It seems to me as if every place were sunny, save Brook Farm. Nevertheless, I had rather a pleasant walk to a distant meadow, a day or two ago; and we found white and purple grapes, in great abundance, ripe, and 54 gushing with rich juice when the hand pressed their clusters. Didst thou know what treasures of wild grapes there are in this land. If we dwell here, we will make our own wine—of which, I know, my Dove will want a great quantity.

Good bye, sweetest. If thou canst contrive to send me a glimpse of sunshine, I will be the gratefullest husband on earth. I love thee inextinguishably. Thou hast no place to put all the love which I feel for thee.

THINE OWNEST
HUSBAND.

Miss Sophia A. Peabody,
Boston, Mass.

TO MISS PEABODY

Brook Farm, Septr. 27th, 1841.
7½ A.M.

Dearest love,

Thy two letters of business came both together, Saturday evening! What an acute and energetic personage is my little Dove! I say it not in jest (though with a smile) but in good earnest, and with a comfortable purpose to commit all my business transactions to thee, when we dwell together. And why dost thou seem to apprehend that thou mayst possibly offend me. Thou canst do so never, but only make me love thee more and more.

Now as to this affair with Munroe. I fully confide in thy opinion that he intends to make an unequal bargain with thy poor simple and innocent husband—never having doubted this, myself. But how is he to accomplish it? I am not, nor shall be, in the least degree in his power; whereas, he is, to a certain extent, in mine. He might announce his projected library, with me for the editor, in all the newspapers in the universe; but still 56 I could not be bound to become the editor, unless by my own act; nor should I have the slightest scruple in refusing to be so, at the last moment, if he persisted in treating me with injustice. Then, as for his printing Grandfather's Chair, I have the copy-right in my own hands, and could and would prevent the sale, or make him account to me for the profits, in case of need. Meantime, he is making arrangements for publishing this library, contracting with other booksellers, and with printers and engravers, and, with every step, making it more difficult for himself to draw back. I, on the other hand, do nothing which I should not do, if the affair with Munroe were at an end; for if I write a book, it will be just as available for some other publisher as for him. My dearest, instead of getting me within his power by this delay, he has trusted to my ignorance and simplicity, and has put *himself* in *my* power. Show the contrary, if thou canst.

He is not insensible of this. At our last interview, he himself introduced the subject of our bargain, and appeared desirous to close it. But thy husband was not prepared, among other reasons, because I do not yet see what materials I shall have for the republications in the library; the works that he has shown me being all ill-adapted for that purpose; and I wish first to see some 57 French and German books, which he has sent for to New York. And, belovedest, before concluding the bargain, I have promised George Hillard to consult him and let him do the business. Is not this consummate discretion? And is not thy husband perfectly safe? Then why does my Dove put herself into a fever? Rather, let her look at the matter with the same perfect composure that I do, who see all around my own position, and know that it is impregnable.

Most sweet wife, I cannot write thee any more at present, as Mr. Ripley is going away instantaneously; but we will talk at length on Saturday, when God means to send me to thee. I love thee infinitely, and admire thee beyond measure, and trust thee in all things, and will never transact any business without consulting thee—though on some rare occasions, it may happen that I will have my own way, after all. I feel inclined to break off this engagement with Munroe; as thou advisest, though not for precisely the reasons thou urgest; but of this hereafter.

THY MOST OWN
HUSBAND.

Miss Sophia A. Peabody,
Care of Dr. N. Peabody,
Boston, Mass.

TO MISS PEABODY

Brook Farm, Septr. 29th, 1841.—A.M.

Ownest wife, I love thee most exceedingly—never so much before; though I am sure I have loved thee through a past eternity. How dost thou do? Dost thou remember that, the day after tomorrow, thou art to meet thy husband? Does thy heart thrill at the thought?

Dearest love, thy husband was elected to two high offices, last night—viz., to be a Trustee of the Brook Farm estate, and Chairman of the Committee of Finance!!!! Now dost thou not blush to have formed so much lower an opinion of my business talents, than is entertained by other discerning people? From the nature of my office, I shall have the chief direction of all the money affairs of the community—the making of bargains—the supervision of receipts and expenditures &c.& c. &c. Thou didst not think of this, when thou didst pronounce me unfit to make a bargain with that petty knave of a publisher. A prophet has 59 no honor among those of his own kindred, nor a financier in the judgment of his wife.

Belovedest, my accession to these august offices does not at all decide the question of my remaining here permanently. I told Mr. Ripley, that I could not spend the winter at the farm, and that it was quite uncertain whether I returned in the spring.

Now, farewell, most dear and sweet wife. Of course, thou canst not expect that a man in eminent public station will have much time to devote to correspondence with a Dove. I will remember thee in the intervals of business, and love thee in all my leisure moments. Will not this satisfy thee?

God bless thee, mine ownest—my treasure—thou gold and diamond of my soul!—my possession forever—my enough and to spare, yet never, never, to be spared! Sweetest, if it should be very stormy on Saturday, expect me not—but the first fair day thereafter.

I put all my love into one kiss, and have twice as much left as before.

THY TRUEST HUSBAND.

Miss Sophia A. Peabody,
Care of Dr. N. Peabody,
Boston, Mass.

TO MISS PEABODY

Brook Farm, Octr. 9th—Before Breakfast [1841]

Most dear,

Here is thy husband trying to write to thee, while it is so dark that he can hardly see his own scribble—not that it is very early; for the sun is up long ago, and ought to be shining into my window. But this dismal gloom! I positively cannot submit to have this precious month all darkened with cloud and sullied with drizzle.

Dearest, I return the manuscript tale. It is pretty enough; but I doubt whether it be particularly suited to the American public; and, if intended for publication, I trust it will undergo a very severe revision. It will need it. I speak frankly about this matter; but I should do the same (only more frankly still) if the translation were my Dove's own.

I wonder whether Munroe has yet returned Grandfather's Chair to Elizabeth. I send back his books to-day. 61

Belovedest, I think thou wilt see me in the latter half of next week. Thou needest not to give up any visit to South Boston on this account; for I cannot get to thee before twelve o'clock. It will be but an hour or so's visit.

Thine with deepest and
keenest love,
THEODORE DE
L'AUBEPINE.

Miss Sophia A. Peabody,
Care of Dr. N. Peabody,
Boston, Mass.

TO MISS PEABODY

Brook Farm, October 18th,
Saturday [1841]

Most dear wife, I received thy letter and note, last night, and was much gladdened by them; for never has my soul so yearned for thee as now. But, belovedest, my spirit is moved to talk to thee to day about these magnetic miracles, and to beseech thee to take no part in them. I am unwilling that a power should be exercised on thee, of which we know neither the origin nor the consequence, and the phenomena of which seem rather calculated to bewilder us, than to teach us any truths about the present or future state of being. If I possessed such a power over thee, I should not dare to exercise it; nor can I consent to its being exercised by another. Supposing that this power arises from the transfusion of one spirit into another, it seems to me that the sacredness of an individual is violated by it; there would be an intrusion into thy holy of holies—and the intruder would not be 63 thy husband! Canst thou think, without a shrinking of thy soul, of any human being coming into closer communion with thee than I may?—than either nature or my own sense of right would permit me? I cannot. And, dearest, thou must remember, too, that thou art now a part of me, and that, by surrendering thyself to the influence of this magnetic lady, thou surrenderest more than thine own moral and spiritual being—allowing that the influence *is* a moral and spiritual one. And, sweetest, I really do not like the idea of being brought, through thy medium, into such an intimate relation with Mrs. Park!

Now, ownest wife, I have no faith whatever that people are raised to the seventh heaven, or to any heaven at all, or that they gain any insight into the mysteries of life beyond death, by means of this strange science. Without distrusting that the phenomena which thou tellest me of, and others as remarkable, have really occurred, I think that they are to be accounted for as the result of a physical and material, not of a spiritual, influence. *Opium* has produced many a brighter vision of heaven (and just as susceptible of proof) than those which thou recountest. They are dreams, my love—and such dreams as thy sweetest fancy, either waking or sleeping, could vastly improve 64 upon. And what delusion can be more lamentable and mischievous, than to mistake the physical and material for the spiritual? What so miserable as to lose the soul's true, though hidden, knowledge and consciousness of heaven, in the mist of an earth-born vision? Thou shalt not do this. If thou wouldst know what heaven is, before thou comest thither hand in hand with thy husband, then retire into the depths of thine own spirit, and thou wilt find it there among holy thoughts and feelings; but do not degrade high Heaven and its inhabitants into any such symbols and forms as those which Miss Larned describes—do not let an earthly effluence from Mrs. Park's corporeal system bewilder thee, and perhaps contaminate something spiritual and sacred. I should as soon think of seeking revelations of the future state in the rottenness of the grave—where so many do seek it.

Belovedest wife, I am sensible that these arguments of mine may appear to have little real weight; indeed, what I write does no sort of justice to what I think. But I care the less for this, because I know that my deep and earnest feeling upon the subject will weigh more with thee than all the arguments in the world. And thou wilt know that the view which I take of this matter is 65 caused by no want of faith in mysteries, but from a deep reverence of the soul, and of the mysteries which it knows within itself, but never transmits to the earthly eye or ear. Keep thy imagination sane—that is one of the truest conditions of communion with Heaven.

Dearest, after these grave considerations, it seems hardly worth while to submit a merely external one; but as it occurs to me, I will write it. I cannot think, without invincible repugnance, of thy holy name being bruited abroad in connection with these magnetic phenomena. Some (horrible thought!) would pronounce my Dove an impostor; the great majority would deem thee crazed; and even the few believers would feel a sort of interest in thee, which it would be anything but pleasant to excite. And what adequate motive can there be for exposing thyself to all this misconception? Thou wilt say, perhaps, that thy visions and experiences would never be known. But Miss Larned's are known to all who choose to listen.

October 19th. Monday.—Most beloved, what a preachment have I made to thee! I love thee, I love thee, I love thee, most infinitely. Love is the true magnetism. What carest thou for any other? Belovedest, it is probable that thou wilt 66 see thy husband tomorrow. Art thou magnificent? God bless thee. What a bright day is here; but the woods are fading now. It is time I were in the city, for the winter..

Miss Sophia A. Peabody,
Care of Dr. N. Peabody,
Boston, Mass.

TO MISS PEABODY

Brook Farm, October 21st, 1841—Noon

Ownest beloved, I know thou dost not care in the least about receiving a word from thy husband—thou lovest me not—in fact thou hast quite forgotten that such a person exists. I do love thee so much, that I really think that all the love is on my side;—there is no room for any more in the whole universe.

Sweetest, I have nothing at all to say to thee—nothing, I mean, that regards this external world; and as to matters of the heart and soul, they are not to be written about. What atrocious weather! In all this month, we have not had a single truly October day; it has been a real November month, and of the most disagreeable kind. I came to this place in one snowstorm, and shall probably leave it in another; so that my reminiscences of Brook Farm are like to be the coldest and dreariest imaginable. But next month, thou, belovedest, will 68 be my sunshine and my summer. No matter what weather it may be then.

Dearest, good bye. Dost thou love me after all? Art thou magnificently well? God bless thee. Thou didst make me infinitely happiest, at our last meeting. Was it a pleasant season likewise to thee?

Thine ownest,
THEODORE DE
L'AUBEPINE.

Miss Sophia A. Peabody,
Care of Dr. N. Peabody,
Boston, Mass.

TO MISS PEABODY

Salem, Novr. 27th, 1841

Dearest Soul,

I know not whether thou wilt have premonitions of a letter from thy husband; but I feel absolutely constrained to write thee a few lines this morning, before I go up in town. I love thee—I love thee—and I have no real existence but in thee. Never before did my bosom so yearn for the want of thee—so thrill at the thought of thee. Thou art a mighty enchantress, my little Dove, and hast quite subdued a strong man, who deemed himself independent of all the world. I am a captive under thy little foot, and look to thee for life. Stoop down and kiss me—or I die!

Dearest, I am intolerably weary of this old town; and I would that my visits might not be oftener than once in ten years, instead of a fortnight. Dost thou not think it really the most hateful place in all the world? My mind becomes heavy and nerveless, the moment I set my 70 foot within its precincts. Nothing makes me wonder more than that I found it possible to write all my tales in this same region of sleepy-head and stupidity. But I suppose the characteristics of the place are reproduced in the tales; and that accounts for the overpowering disposition to slumber which so many people experience, in reading thy husband's productions.

Belovedest, according to thy instructions, I have been very careful in respect to mince-pies and other Thanksgiving dainties; and so have passed pretty well through the perils of the carnival season. Thou art a dearest little wife, and I would live on bread and water, to please thee, even if such temperate regimen should produce no other good. But truly thou art very wise in thy dietetic rules; and it is well that I have such a wife to take care of me; inasmuch as I am accustomed to eat whatever is given me, with an appetite as indiscriminate, though not quite so enormous, as that of an ostrich. Setting aside fat pork, I refuse no other Christian meat.

Dearest, I write of nothing; for I had nothing to write when I began, save to make thee aware that I loved thee infinitely; and now that thou knowest it, there is no need of saying a word more. On Monday evening, please God, I shall see thee. 71 How would I have borne it, if thy visit to Ida Russel were to commence before my return to thine arms?

God bless thee, mine ownest.

THY TRUEST HUSBAND.

Miss Sophia A. Peabody,
Care of Dr. N. Peabody,
Boston, Mass.

TO MISS PEABODY

72

54 Pinckney St., Jany. 1st, [1842]

Very dearest,

I would gladly go to Salem immediately if I could, but I am detained here by some ceremonies, which are needful to be gone through, previous to my final deliverance from the Custom-House. As Mr. Bancroft is not expected back from Washington for some days, I shall probably remain till nearly the close of next week. Meantime, I must be near at hand, because my presence may be required at any moment.

Naughtiest, thou shouldst not put thy little white hands into cold clay. Canst thou not use warm water? How canst thou hope for any warmth of conception and execution, when thou art working with material as cold as ice?

As to the proof-sheets, I think we need not trouble.... (Remainder of letter missing)

TO MISS PEABODY

Truest Heart,

Here is thy husband in his old chamber, where he produced those stupendous works of fiction, which have since impressed the Universe with wonderment and awe! To this chamber, doubtless, in all succeeding ages, pilgrims will come to pay their tribute of reverence;—they will put off their shoes at the threshold, for fear of desecrating the tattered old carpet. "There," they will exclaim, "is the very bed in which he slumbered, and where he was visited by those ethereal visions, which he afterward fixed forever in glowing words! There is the wash-stand, at which this exalted personage cleansed himself from the stains of earth, and rendered his outward man a fitting exponent of the pure soul within. There, in its mahogany frame, is the dressing-glass, which reflected that noble brow, those hyacinthine locks, that mouth, bright with smiles, or tremulous with 74 feeling, that flashing or melting eye, that—in short, every item of the magnanimous phiz of this unexampled man! There is the pine table—there the old flag-bottomed chair—in which he sat, and at which he scribbled, during his agonies of inspiration! There is the old chest of drawers, in which he kept what shirts a poor author may be supposed to have possessed! There is the closet, in which was reposited his threadbare suit of black! There is the worn-out shoe-brush with which this polished writer polished his boots. There is—" but I believe this will be pretty much all;—so here I close the catalogue.

Most dear, I love thee beyond all limits, and write to thee because I cannot help it;—nevertheless, writing grows more and more an inadequate and unsatisfactory mode of revealing myself to thee. I no longer think of saying anything deep, because I feel that the deepest and truest must remain unsaid. We have left expression—at least, such expression as can be achieved with pen and ink—far behind us. Even the spoken word has long been inadequate. Looks are a better language; but, bye-and-bye, our spirits will demand some more adequate expression even than these. And thus it will go on; until we shall be divested of these earthly forms, which are at once our medium 75 of expression, and the impediments to full communion. Then we shall melt into [one] another, and all be expressed, once and continually, without a word—without an effort.

Belovedest, my cold is very comfortable now. Mrs. Hillard gave me some homo—I don't know how to spell it—homeopathic medicine, of which I took a dose last night; and shall not need another. Art thou likewise well? Didst thou weary thy poor little self to death, yesterday? I do not think that I could possibly undergo the fatigue and distraction of mind which thou dost. Thou art ten times as powerful as I, because thou art so much more ethereal.

Sweetest, thy husband has recently been both lectured about and preached about, here in his native city. The preacher was Rev. Mr. Fox of Newburyport; but how he contrived to hook me into a sermon, I know not. I trust he took for his text that which was spoken of my namesake of old—"Behold an Israelite indeed, in whom there is no guile." Belovedest, if ever thou shouldst happen to hear me lauded on any public occasion, I shall expect thee to rise, and make thine own and my acknowledgments, in a neat and appropriate speech. Wilt thou not? Surely thou wilt—inasmuch as I care little for applause, save as it 76 shall please thee; so it is rather thy concern than mine.

Mine ownest, it is by no means comfortable to be separated from thee three whole days at a time. It is too great a gap in life. There is no sunshine in the days in which thou dost not shine on me. And speaking of sunshine, what a beautifullest day (to the outward eye, I mean) was yesterday; and to-day seems equally bright and gladsome, although I have not yet tasted the fresh air. I trust that thou has flown abroad, and soared upward to the seventh heaven. But do not stay there, sweetest Dove! Come back for me; for I shall never get there, unless by the aid of thy wings.

Now God bless thee, and make thee happy and joyful, until Saturday evening, when thou must needs bear the infliction of

THINE OWNEST
HUSBAND.

Miss Sophia A. Peabody,
Care of Dr. N. Peabody,
Boston, Mass.

TO MISS PEABODY

Salem, Feby. 27th, 1842—
Forenoon

Thou dearest Heart,

As it is uncertain whether I shall return to Boston tomorrow, I write thee a letter; for I need to commune with thee; and even if I should bring the scroll of my thoughts and feelings with me, perhaps thou wilt not refuse to receive it. It is awful, almost (and yet I would not have it otherwise, for the world) to feel how necessary thou hast become to my well-being, and how my spirit is disturbed at a separation from thee, and stretches itself out through the dimness and distance to embrace its other self. Thou art my quiet and satisfaction—not only my chiefest joy, but the condition of all other enjoyments. When thou art away, vague fears and misgivings sometimes steal upon me; there are heart-quakes and spirit-sinkings for no real cause, and which never trouble me when thou art with me.

Belovedest, I have thought much of thy parting 78 injunction to tell my mother and sisters that thou art her daughter and their sister. I do not think that thou canst estimate what a difficult task thou didst propose to me—not that any awful and tremendous effect would be produced by the disclosure; but because of the strange reserve, in regard to matters of feeling, that has always existed among us. We are conscious of one another's feelings, always; but there seems to be a tacit law, that our deepest heart-concernments are not to be spoken of. I cannot gush out in their presence—I cannot take my heart in my hand, and show it to them. There is a feeling within me (though I know it is a foolish one) as if it would be as indecorous to do so, as to display to them the naked breast. And they are in the same state as myself. None, I think, but delicate and sensitive persons could have got into such a position; but doubtless this incapacity of free communion, in the hour of especial need, is meant by Providence as a retribution for something wrong in our early intercourse.

Then it is so hard to speak of thee—*really* of thee—to anybody! I doubt whether I ever have *really* spoken of thee to any person. I have spoken the name of Sophia, it is true; but the idea in my mind was apart from thee—it embraced nothing of thine inner and essential self; it was an 79 outward and faintly-traced shadow that I summoned up, to perform thy part, and which I placed in the midst of thy circumstances; so that thy sister Mary, or Mrs. Ripley, or even Margaret, were deceived, and fancied that I was talking about thee. But there didst thou lie, thy real self, in my deepest, deepest heart, while far above, at the surface, this distant image of thee was the subject of talk. And it was not without an effort which few are capable of making, that I could ever do so much; and even then I felt as if it were profane. Yet I spoke to persons from whom, if from any, I might expect true sympathy in regard to thee.

I tell thee these things, in order that my Dove, into whose infinite depths the sunshine falls continually, may perceive what a cloudy veil stretches over the abyss of my nature. Thou wilt not think that it is caprice or stubbornness that has made me hitherto resist thy wishes. Neither. I think, is it a love of secrecy and darkness. I am glad to think that God sees through my heart; and if any angel has power to penetrate into it, he is welcome to know everything that is there. Yes; and so may any mortal, who is capable of full sympathy, and therefore worthy to come into my depths. But he must find his own way there. I 80 can neither guide him nor enlighten him. It is this involuntary reserve, I suppose, that has given the objectivity to my writings. And when people think that I am pouring myself out in a tale or essay, I am merely telling what is common to human nature, not what is peculiar to myself. I sympathise with them—not they with me.

Feb. 28th—Forenoon.—Sweetest, thou shalt have this letter instead of thy husband, to-night. Dost thou love me? I shall not find any letter from thee at the Post Office, because thou dost expect to hear my footsteps on thy staircase, at six o'clock this evening. Oh, but another day will quickly pass; and then this yearning of the soul will be appeased, for a little while at least. I wonder, I wonder, I wonder, where on earth we are to set up our tabernacle. God knows;—but I want to know too.

Dearest love, I am very well, and comfortable as I desire to be, in thy absence. After all, it is a happiness to need thee, to sigh for thee, to feel the nothingness of all things without thee. But do not thou think so—thou must be happy always, not independently of thy husband, but with a bliss equally pervading presence and absence.

Belovedest, I have employed most of my time here in collecting curiosities, and have so many on 81 my hands that I begin to fear it will require a volume to contain the catalogue. I would we had such a museum in reality. And now good-bye, most true Heart. Methinks this is the longest letter that I have written thee for a great while. Shalt thou expect me to write during my journey to New York?—or, were it not better to allow thee to forget me entirely, during that interval of a week? God bless thee, thou unforgettablest and unforgettingest,

THINE OWNEST
HUSBAND.

Miss Sophia A. Peabody,
Care of Dr. N. Peabody,
13 West-street,
Boston, Mass.

TO MISS PEABODY

82

New York, March 4th, 1842

Dearest, I can find only this torn sheet of paper, on which to scribble thee a bulletin. We are arrived safely; but I am very homesick for thee—otherwise well and in good spirits. I love thee infinitely much. Belovedest, I know not whether the Colonel and I will leave this city on Monday or Tuesday, but if thou hast not already written, it will be to[o] late to direct a letter hither. In that case, best wife, write to Albany—whence I shall write to thee. The steam-engine kept me awake last night; but I cared not, for I was thinking about thee.

I am exceedingly well.

Dost thou love me?
HUSBAND.

Miss Sophia A. Peabody,
Care of Dr. N. Peabody,
Boston, Mass.

TO MISS PEABODY

Mine own Heart, I arrived here early this morning, by the steamboat; and thou mayst be well assured that I lost no time in going to the Post Office; and never did even a letter from thee so thrill my heart as this. There is no expressing what I feel; and so I will not try—especially now when I am compelled to write in a bar-room with people talking and drinking around me. But I love thee a thousand infinities more than ever.

Most dear, I have come hither to see Mr. O'Sullivan, with whom I have relations of business as well as friendship, all which thou shalt know, if thou thinkest them worth enquiring about. The good colonel is with me; but is going about a hundred miles into the interior, tomorrow. In the meantime I shall remain here; but thou wilt see me again on Tuesday evening. How is it possible to wait so long? It is not possible—yet I have much to talk of with O'Sullivan; and this 84 will be the longest absence that we shall be compelled to endure, before the time when thou shalt be the companion of all my journeys.

Truest wife, it is possible that the cars may not arrive in Boston till late in the evening; but I have good hope to be with thee by six o'clock, or a little after, on Tuesday. God bless us.

Miss Sophia A. Peabody,
Care of Dr. N. Peabody,
Boston, Mass.

TO MISS PEABODY

Salem, Wednesday, April 5th, 1842

My Dear,

It was thy husband's intention to spend all his leisure time, here at home, in sketching out a tale; but my spirit demands communion with thine so earnestly, that I must needs write to thee, if all the affairs in the world were pressing on me at once. My breast is full of thee; thou art throbbing throughout all my veins. Never, it seems to me, did I know what love was, before. And yet I am not satisfied to let that sentence pass; for it would do wrong to the blissful and holy time that we have already enjoyed together. But our hearts are new-created for one another daily, and they enter upon existence with such up-springing rapture as if nothing had ever existed before—as if, at this very *now*, the physical and spiritual world were but first discovered, and by ourselves only. This is Eternity—thus will every moment of forever-and-ever be the first moment of life, and no weariness can gather upon us from the past.

It is a bliss which I never wish to enjoy, when I can attain that of thy presence; but it is nevertheless 86 a fact, that there is a bliss even in being absent from thee. This yearning that disturbs my very breath—this earnest stretching out of my soul towards thee—this voice of my heart, calling for thee out of its depths, and complaining that thou art not instantly given to it—all these are a joy; for they make me know how entirely our beings have blended into one another. After all, these pangs are but symptoms of the completeness of our spiritual union—the effort of the outward to respond to the inward. Dearest, I do not express myself clearly on this matter; but what need?—wilt not thou know better what I mean than words could tell thee? Dost not thou too rejoice in everything that gives thee a more vivid consciousness that we are one?—even if it have something like pain in it. The desire of my soul is to know thee continually, and to know that thou art mine; and absence, as well as presence, gives me this knowledge—and as long as I have it, I live. It is, indeed, impossible for us ever to be really absent from one another; the only absence, for those who love, is estrangement or forgetfulness—and we can never know what those words mean. Oh, dear me, my mind writes nonsense, because it is an insufficient interpreter for my heart. 87

... Most beloved, I am thinking at this moment of thy dearest nose! Thou canst not know how infinitely better I know and love Sophie Hawthorne, since she has yielded up that fortress. And, in requital, I yield my whole self up to her, and kiss her beloved foot, and acknowledge her for my queen and liege-lady forever more. Come into my heart, dearest; for I am about to close my letter. Hitherto, I have kept thee at arms' length; because the very act of writing necessarily supposes that thou art apart from me; but now I throw down the pen, in order that thou mayst be the closer to me.

> Thine ownest Husband,
> NATH. HAWTHORNE.

Miss Sophia A. Peabody,
Care of Dr. N. Peabody,
Boston, Mass.

TO MISS PEABODY

54 Pinckney St., Monday,
11 o'clock A.M. [1842]

Most dear love,

I have been caught by a personage who has been in search of me for two or three days, and shall be compelled to devote this unfortunate evening to him, instead of to my Dove. Dost thou regret it?—so does thy poor husband, who loves thee infinitely, and needs thee continually. Art thou well to-day very dearest? How naughty was I, last night, to contend against thy magnetic influence, and turn it against thyself! I will not do so again. My head has been in pain for thine—at least my heart has. Thou wast very sweet and lovely, last night—so art thou always.

Belovedest, thou knowest not how I yearn for thee—how I long and pray for the time when we may be together without disturbance—when absence shall be a rare exception to our daily life. My heart will blossom like a rose, when it can be 89 always under thy daily influence—when the dew of thy love will be falling upon it, every moment.

Most sweet, lest I should not be able to avoid another engagement for tomorrow evening, I think it best for me to come in the afternoon—shortly after two o'clock, on Tuesday. Canst thou devote so much of thy precious day to my unworthiness? Unless I hear from thee, I shall come. I love thee. I love thee.

Dearest, I kiss thee with my whole spirit.

Thy husband,
THEODORE DE
L'AUBEPINE.

Miss Sophia A. Peabody,
Care of Dr. N. Peabody,
Boston, Mass.

TO MISS PEABODY

54 Pinckney St., May 19th
[1842]

My Ownest,

Mr. Hillard, this morning, put into my hands the enclosed paragraph from the Philadelphia Saturday Courier. It is to be hoped that the penny papers of this city will copy an item of so much public importance.

Canst thou tell me whether the "Miss Peabody" here mentioned, is Miss Mary or Miss Elizabeth Peabody?

P.S. Please to present my congratulations to the "accomplished Miss Peabody." But I shall call, this evening, and present them in person.

Miss Sophia A. Peabody,
13 West-street,
Boston.

TO MISS PEABODY

54 Pinckney St., May 27th, 1842

Dearest Heart,

Thy letter to my sisters was most beautiful—sweet, gentle, and magnanimous; such as no angel save my Dove, could have written. If they do not love thee, it will be because they have no hearts to love with;—and even if this were the case, I should not despair of thy planting the seeds of hearts in their bosoms. They will love thee, all in good time, dearest; and we will be very happy. I am so at this moment, while my breast heaves with the consciousness of what a treasure God has given me—in whom I see more to worship, and admire, and love, every day of my life; and shall see more and more as long as I live; else, it will be because my own nature retrogrades, instead of advancing. But thou wilt make me better and better, till I am even worthy to be thy husband.

Oh, truest wife, what a long widowhood is this! Three evenings without a glimpse of thee! And I know not whether I am to come at six or seven 92 o'clock tomorrow evening—or scarcely, indeed, whether I am to come at all. But, unless thou orderest me to the contrary, I shall come at seven o'clock.

I met Mr. Emerson at the Athenaeum yesterday. He tells me that our garden, &c., makes fine progress. Would that we were there. God bless us.

Miss Sophia A. Peabody,
No. 13 West-street,
Boston.

TO MISS PEABODY

Dearest wife,

I love thee beyond all hope of expression—so do thou measure it by thine own love for me, if indeed thou canst continue to love me, after our parting. But never did I love thee better than then; and I am even glad that this vapor of tobacco smoke did, for once, roll thus darkly and densely between us, because it helps me to hate the practice forevermore. Thou wast very sweet not to scold me fiercely, for allowing myself to be so impregnated.

Sweetest, scarcely had I arrived here, when our mother came out of her chamber, looking better and more cheerful than I have seen her this some time, and enquired about the health and well-being of my Dove! Very kindly too. Then was thy husband's heart much lightened; for I knew that almost every agitating circumstance of her life had hitherto cost her a fit of sickness; and I 94 knew not but it might be so now. Foolish me, to doubt that my mother's love would be wise, like all other genuine love! And foolish again, to have doubted my Dove's instinct—whom, henceforth—(if never before)—I take for my unerring guide and counsellor in all matters of the heart and soul. Yet if, sometimes, I should perversely follow mine own follies, do not thou be discouraged. I shall always acknowledge thy superior wisdom in the end; and, I trust, not too late for it to exert its good influence. Now I am very happy—happier than my naughtiness deserves. It seems that our mother had seen how things were, a long time ago. At first, her heart was troubled, because she knew that much of outward as well as inward fitness was requisite to secure thy foolish husband's peace; but, gradually and quietly, God has taught her that all is good; and so, thou dearest wife, we shall have her fullest blessing and concurrence. My sisters, too, begin to sympathise as they ought; and all is well. God be praised! I thank Him on my knees, and pray him to make me worthy of thee, and of the happiness thou bringest me.

Mine ownest, I long for thee, yet bear our separation patiently, because time and space, and all other finite obstructions, are so fast flitting away 95 from between us. We can already measure the interval by days and hours. What bliss!—and what awe is intermingled with it!—no fear nor doubt, but a holy awe, as when an immortal spirit is drawing near to the gate of Heaven. I cannot tell what I feel; but thou knowest it all.

Sweetest, it is my purpose to remain here till Friday, when, unless thou forbiddest me, I shall be with thee at seven o'clock. God bless thee! I have no more words, but a heart full of love.

THINE OWNEST
HUSBAND.

Miss Sophia A. Peabody,
Care of Dr. N. Peabody,
Boston, Mass.

TO MISS PEABODY

True and Honorable Wife,

Thou hast not been out of mind a moment since I saw thee last,—and never wilt thou be, so long as we exist. Canst thou say as much? Dearest, dost thou know that there are but ten days more in this blessed month of June? And dost thou remember what is to happen within those ten days? Poor little Dove! Now dost thou tremble, and shrink back, and beginnest to fear that thou hast acted too rashly in this matter. Now dost thou say to thyself—"Oh, that I could prevail upon this wretched person to allow me a month or two longer to make up my mind; for, after all, he is but an acquaintance of yesterday; and unwise am I, to give up father, mother, and sisters, for the sake of such a questionable stranger!" Ah, foolish virgin! It is too late; nothing can part us now; for God Himself hath ordained that we shall be one. So nothing remains, but to reconcile thyself to thy destiny. Year by year, thou must come closer and closer to me; and a thousand 97 ages hence, we shall be only in the honeymoon of our marriage. Poor little Dove!

Sweetest wife, I cannot write to thee. The time for that species of communion is past. Hereafter, I cannot write my feelings, but only external things, business, facts, details, matters which do not relate to the heart and soul, but merely to our earthly condition. I have long had such a feeling, whenever I took up my pen—and now more than ever.

Would that I knew when the priest is to thrust himself between us! Dearest, the last day of the month, if I mistake not, is Thursday, of next week. Unless thou desirest my presence sooner, I shall return to Boston probably on Sunday evening. Then will the days lag heavily, till we can flee away and be at rest. And, I pray thee, let our flight be in the morning; for it would be strange and wearisome to live half a day of ordinary life at such an epoch. I should be like a body walking about the city without a soul—being therein the reverse of good old Dr. Harris, whose soul walks about without the body. And this reminds me, that he has not made himself visible of late. Foolish me, not to have accosted him; for perhaps he wished to give us some good advice on our entrance into connubial life—or possibly, he intended to disclose the hiding-place of some ancient 98 hoard of gold, which would have freed us forever from all pecuniary cares. I think we shall not need his counsel on the former point; but on the latter, it would have been peculiarly acceptable.

Ownest, would there be anything amiss in exchanging that copy of Southey's Poems for some other book? We should still have Campbell's English Poets as an immediate keepsake from Miss Burley; and whatever book we might procure would be none the less a gift from her. My copy of Southey went to the Manse with my furniture; else I should have brought it hither and given it to Elizabeth—who, however, does not especially admire Southey.

Now good bye, dearest love. I fear thou wilt make thyself sick with much care and toil. God bless thee! Our mother and sisters would send their love, if they knew that I am writing to thee. They love thee, and link us together in their thoughts. God bless them, and us, and everybody. Dost thou perceive how love widens my heart?

Miss Sophia A. Peabody,
Care of Dr. N. Peabody,
Boston, Mass.

TO MISS PEABODY

Boston, June 24th.—past 8
o'clock P.M. [1842]

Mine ownest,

I have just received thy letter, and rejoice unspeakably at the news which thou tellest me. Dearest, thou knowest not how I have yearned for thee during thy absence; and yet thou didst seem so well and happy there, that I sent thee a letter, yesterday morning, submitting it to thy wisdom whether thou hadst not better stay another week. But thou hast done more wisely to come; for my heart is faint with hunger for thee. I have been quite sad and dolorous at thy absence. And oh, what joy to think that henceforth there shall be no long separations for us. It has taken me so by surprise that I know not what to say upon the subject; but my heart throbs mightily.

Dearest, thou canst not have a long letter to-night, because thy husband is weary, and moreover he wants to think about thee, and embrace thee a thousand million times deep within himself. 100 Art thou quite well? Most beloved, I beseech [thee] not to agitate thyself in this removal of the household gods. I shall come on Saturday, but perhaps not till late. God bless and keep thee.

Thine ownest, lovingest
husband,
DE L'AUBEPINE.

Miss Sophia A. Peabody,
Care of Dr. N. Peabody,
Salem, Mass.

TO MISS PEABODY

54 Pinckney St., June 27th. —7
o'clock P.M. [1842]

Most Dear,

I have just arrived from Salem, and find thy note, in which thou tellest me of thy illness. Oh, my poor little Dove, thou dost need a husband with a strong will to take care of thee; and when I have the charge of thee, thou wilt find thyself under much stricter discipline than ever before. How couldst thou be so imprudent? Yet I will not scold thee till thou art quite well. Then thou must look for scoldings and chastisement too.

Belovedest, I shall not say a single word to induce thee to go through the ceremony on Monday;—nay I do not know that I will consent to its taking place then. This we will determine upon tomorrow evening. If thou art not very well indeed, I shall be afraid to take thee from under thy mother's care. And, belovedest, do not fear but that I will bear patiently any necessary delay—and 102 I know that thou wilt recover as soon as possible, for my sake.

Dearest, God bless thee. Keep thy heart quiet; and tomorrow evening we will meet in hope and joy.

THY LOVINGEST
HUSBAND.

Miss Sophia A. Peabody,
13 West-street,
Boston.

TO MISS PEABODY

54 Pinckney St.—June 30th.—
morning [1842]

Dearest Love,

Thy sister Mary, after I left thee, told me that it was her opinion that we should not be married for a week longer. I had hoped, as thou knowest, for an earlier day; but I cannot help feeling that Mary is on the safe and reasonable side. Shouldst thou feel that this postponement is advisable, thou wilt find me patient beyond what thou thinkest me capable of. I will even be happy, if thou wilt only keep thy mind and heart in peace.

Belovedest, didst thou sleep well, last night? My pillow was haunted with ghastly dreams, the details whereof have flitted away like vapors, but a strong impression remains about thy being magnetised. God save me from any more such! I awoke in an absolute quake. Dearest, I cannot oppose thy submitting to so much of this influence as will relieve thy headache; but, as thou lovest me, do not suffer thyself to be put to sleep. My 104 feeling on this point is so strong, that it would be wronging us both to conceal it from thee.

My ownest, if it will at all reconcile thee to the ceremony, I will go to Concord, tomorrow or next day, and see about our affairs there. I would even go there and live alone, if thou didst bid me though I shall be much happier in lingering here, and visiting thy couch every evening, and hearing thee say that thou art better than the night before.

What a sweet morning is this; it makes me feel bright and hopeful, after the troubles of the night.

THINE   OWNEST
HUSBAND.

P.S. I enclose an order for a case of mine, which is to be given to the baggage-wagoner, when he comes for the furniture. He can present it, and receive the case.

P.S. 2d. I love thee! I love thee! I love thee.

P.S. 3d. Dost thou love me at all?

Miss Sophia A. Peabody,
13 West-street,
Boston.

TO MRS. HAWTHORNE

Salem, March 12th (Saturday), 1843

Own wifie, how dost thou do? I have been in some anxiety about thy little head, and indeed about the whole of thy little person. Art thou ill at ease in any mode whatever? I trust that thy dearest soul will not be quite worn out of thee, with the activity and bustle of thy present whereabout, so different from the intense quiet of our home. That poor home! How desolate it is now! Last night, being awake, my thoughts travelled back to the lonely old house; and it seemed as if I was wandering up stairs and down stairs all by myself. My fancy was almost afraid to be there, alone. I could see every object in a sort of dim, gray light—our bed-chamber—the study, all in confusion—the parlor, with the fragments of that abortive breakfast on the table, and the precious silver-forks, and the old bronze image keeping its solitary stand upon the mantel-piece. Then, methought, the wretched Pigwigger came 106 and jumped upon the window-sill, and clung there with her forepaws, mewing dismally for admittance, which I could not grant her, being there myself only in the spirit. And then came the ghost of the old Doctor stalking through the gallery, and down the staircase, and peeping into the parlor; and though I was wide awake, and conscious of being so many miles from the spot, still it was quite awful to think of the ghost having sole possession of our home; for I could not quite separate myself from it, after all. Somehow, the Doctor and I seemed to be there tete-a-tete, and I wanted thee to protect me. Why wast not thou there in thought, at the same moment; and then we should have been conscious of one another, and have had no fear, and no desolate feeling. I believe I did not have any fantasies about the ghostly kitchen-maid; but I trust Mary left the flat-irons within her reach; so that she may do all the ironing while we are away, and never disturb us more at midnight. I suppose she comes thither to iron her shroud, and perhaps, likewise, to smooth the doctor's band. Probably, during her lifetime, she allowed the poor old gentleman to go to some ordination or other grand clerical celebration with rumpled linen, and ever since, and throughout all earthly futurity (at least, so long 107 us the house shall stand) she is doomed to exercise a nightly toil, with spiritual flat-irons. Poor sinner—and doubtless Satan heats the irons for her. What nonsense is all this!—but really, it does make me shiver to think of that poor house of ours. Glad am I that thou art not there without thy husband.

I found our mother tolerably well; and Louisa, I think, in especial good condition for her, and Elizabeth comfortable, only not quite thawed. They speak of thee and me with an evident sense that we are very happy indeed, and I can see that they are convinced of my having found the very little wife that God meant for me. I obey thy injunctions, as well as I can, in my deportment towards them; and though mild and amiable manners are foreign to my nature, still I get along pretty well for a new beginner. In short, they seem content with thy husband, and I am very certain of their respect and affection for his wife.

Take care of thy little self, I tell thee! I praise heaven for this snow and "slosh," because it will prevent thee from scampering all about the city, as otherwise thou wouldst infallibly have done. Lie abed late—sleep during the day—go to bed seasonably—refuse to see thy best friend, if either flesh or spirit be sensible of the slightest repugnance—drive 108 all trouble out of thy mind—and above all things, think continually what an admirable husband thou hast! So shalt thou have quiet sleep and happy awaking; and when I fold thee to my bosom again, thou wilt be such a round, rosy, smiling little dove, that I shall feel as if I had grasped all cheerfulness and sunshine within the span of thy waist.

Mrs. Sophia A. Hawthorne,
Care of Dr. N. Peabody,
Boston, Mass.

TO MRS. HAWTHORNE

Dearest wife, Thy letters have all been received; and I know not that I could have kept myself alive without them; for never was my heart so hungry and tired as it is now. I need thee continually wherever I am, and nothing else makes any approach towards satisfying me. Thou hast the easier part—being drawn out of thyself by society; but with me there is an ever-present yearning, which nothing outward seems to have any influence upon. Four whole days must still intervene before we meet—it is too long—too long—we have not so much time to spare out of eternity.

As for this Mr. Billings, I wish he would not be so troublesome. I put a note for him into the Boston Post-Office, directed according to his own request. His scheme is well enough, and might possibly become popular; but it has no peculiar advantages with reference to myself; nor do the subjects of his proposed books particularly suit my fancy, as themes to write upon. Somebody else 110 will answer his purpose just as well; and I would rather write books of my own imagining than be hired to develope the ideas of an engraver; especially as the pecuniary prospect is not better, nor so good, as it might be elsewhere. I intend to adhere to my former plan, of writing one or two mythological story books, to be published under O'Sullivan's auspices in New York—which is the only place where books can be published, with a chance of profit. As a matter of courtesy, I may perhaps call on Mr. Billings, if I have time; but I do not intend to be connected with this affair.

It is queer news that thou tellest me about the Pioneer. I expected it to fail in due season, but not quite so soon. Shouldst there be an opportunity within a day or two, I wish thou wouldst send for any letters that may be in the Post-Office there; but not unless some person is going thither, with intent to return before Wednesday next. If thou receive any, keep them till we meet in Boston.

I dreamed the other night that our house was broken open, and all our silver stolen. No matter though it be:—we have steel forks and German silver spoons in plenty, and I only wish that we were to eat our dinner with them to-day. But we shall have gained nothing on the score of snow, and slosh, and mud, by our absence; for the bad 111 walking will be at its very *ne plus ultra*, next week. Wouldst thou not like to stay just one little fortnight longer in Boston, where the sidewalks afford dry passage to thy little feet? It will be mid-May, at least, ere thou wilt find even tolerable walking in Concord. So if thou wishest to walk while thou canst, we will put off our return a week longer. Naughty husband that I am! I know by my own heart that thou pinest for our home, and for the bosom where thou belongest. A week longer! It is a horrible thought.

We cannot very well afford to buy a surplus stock of paper, just now. By and by, I should like some, and I suppose there will always be opportunities to get it cheap at auction. I do wonder—and always shall wonder, until the matter be reformed—why Providence keeps us so short of cash. Our earnings are miserably scanty at best; yet, if we could but get even that pittance, I should continue to be thankful, though certainly for small favors. The world deserves to come to a speedy end, if it were for nothing else save to break down the abominable system of credit—of keeping possession of other people's property—which renders it impossible for a man to be just and honest, even if so inclined. It is almost a pity that the comet is retrograding from the earth; it might do away with all our perversities at one 112 smash. And thou, my little dove, and thy husband for thy sake, might be pretty certain of a removal to some sphere where we should have all our present happiness, and none of these earthly inconveniences.

Ah, but, for the present, I like this earth better than Paradise itself. I love thee, thou dearest. It is only when away from thee, that the chill winds of the world make me shiver. Thou always keepest me warm, and always wilt; and without thee, I should shiver in Heaven. Dearest, I think I prefer to write thy name "Mrs. Sophia A. Hawthorne," rather than "Mrs. Nathaniel Hawthorne";—the latter gives me an image of myself in petticoats, knitting a stocking. I feel so sensibly that thou art my chastest, holiest wife—a *woman* and an angel. But thou dost not love to blush in the midst of people.

Ownest, expect me next Tuesday in the forenoon; and do not look for another letter. I pray heaven that I may find thee well, and not tired quite to death. Even shouldst thou be so, however, I will restore thee on Wednesday.

Mrs. Nathaniel Hawthorne,
Care of Dr. N. Peabody,
Boston, Mass.

TO MRS. HAWTHORNE

Salem, Decr. 2^d, 1844

Ownest Phoebe,

Thy letter came this morning—much needed; for I was feeling desolate and fragmentary. Thou shouldst not ask me to come to Boston, because I can hardly resist setting off this minute—and I have no right to spend money for such luxuries. I think I shall stay here until Bridge reaches Boston; for he wishes to see me then; and, if he could meet thee, and baby, and me, it would save him and us the trouble and perplexity of a visit at Concord. He will probably be in Boston in not much more or less than a week; and I have written to him to call at 13, West St. When he arrives, let him be told to send for me forthwith, or do thou write thyself; and I will immediately make my appearance. Sweetest wife, it goes against my conscience to add another inhabitant to the immense multitude in thy mother's caravanserai; nevertheless, methinks I may come there for one 114 night, and, if I stay longer, remove thence to George Hillard's. But I don't know. I should like to spend two or three days in Boston, if it could be done without any derangement of other people or myself; but I should not feel easy in the caravanserai. Perhaps it would be better to go at once to George Hillard's. After we get home, we will rest one another from all toils.

I am very well, dearest, and it seems to me that I am recovering some of the flesh that I lost, during our long Lent. I do not eat quite enough to satisfy mother and Louisa; but thou wouldst be perfectly satisfied, and so am I. My spirits are pretty equable, though there is a great vacuity caused by thy absence out of my daily life—a bottomless abyss, into which all minor contentments might be flung without filling it up. Still, I feel as if our separation were only apparent—at all events, we are at less than an hour's distance from one another, and therefore may find it easier to spend a week apart. The good that I get by remaining here, is a temporary freedom from that vile burthen which had irked and chafed me so long—that consciousness of debt, and pecuniary botheration, and the difficulty of providing even for the day's wants. This trouble does not pursue me here; and even when we go back, I hope 115 not to feel it nearly so much as before. Polk's election has certainly brightened our prospects; and we have a right to expect that our difficulties will vanish, in the course of a few months.

I long to see our little Una; but she is not yet a vital portion of my being. I find that her idea merges in thine. I wish for thee; and our daughter is included in that wish, without being particularly expressed. She has quite conquered the heart of our mother and sisters; and I am glad of it, for now they can transfer their interest from their own sombre lives to her happy one; and so be blest through her. To confess the truth, she is a dear little thing.

Sweetest Phoebe: I don't intend to stay here more than a week, even if Bridge should not arrive;—and should there be any reason for our returning to Concord sooner, thou canst let me know. Otherwise, I purpose to come to Boston in a week from to-day or tomorrow,—to spend two or three days there—and then go back to the old Abbey; of which there is a very dismal picture at present in my imagination, cold, lonely, and desolate, with untrodden snow along the avenue, and on the doorsteps. But its heart will be warm, when we are within. If thou shalt want me sooner, write,—if not so soon, write. 116

God bless thee, mine ownest. I must close the letter now, because it is dinner-time; and I shall take it to the Post-Office immediately after dinner. I spend almost all my afternoons at the Athenaeum. Kiss our child for me—one kiss for thyself and me together. I love her, and live in thee.

Mrs. Sophia A. Hawthorne,
Care of Dr. N. Peabody,
Boston, Mass.

TO MRS. HAWTHORNE

117

[December, 1844]

Darlingest Phoebe,

I knew that a letter must come to-day; and it cheered and satisfied me, as mine did thee. How we love one another! Blessed we! What a blot I have made of that word "blessed"!

But the consciousness of bliss is as clear as crystal in my heart, though now and then, in great stress of earthly perplexities, a mist bedims its surface.

Belovedest, it will not be anywise necessary for thee to see Bridge at all, before I come,—nor then either, if thou preferrest meeting him in Concord. If I find him resolved to go to Concord, at any rate, I shall not bring him to see thee in Boston; because, as a lady ought, thou appearest to best advantage in thine own house. I merely asked him to call at 13 West-street to learn my whereabout—not to be introduced to thee. Indeed; I should prefer thy not seeing him till I come. It was his purpose to be in Boston before this time; 118 but probably he has remained in Washington to see the opening of Congress, and perhaps to try whether he can help forward our official enterprises. Unless he arrive sooner, I purpose to remain here till Wednesday, and to leave on the evening of that day.

I have not yet called on the Pickmen or the Feet, but solemnly purpose so to do, before I leave Salem.

Mr. Upham, it is said, has resigned his pastorship. When he returned from Concord, he told the most pitiable stories about our poverty and misery; so as almost to make it appear that we were suffering for food. Everybody that speaks to me seems tacitly to take it for granted that we are in a very desperate condition, and that a government office is the only alternative of the almshouse. I care not for the reputation of being wealthier than I am; but we never have been quite paupers, and need not have been represented as such.

Now good-bye, mine ownest little wife! I thank God above all things that thou art my wife—next that Una is our child. I shall come back to thee with tenfold as much love as ever I felt before. Nobody but we ever knew what it is to be married. We alone know the bliss and the 119 mystery; if other people knew it, this dull old earth would have a perpetual glow round about it.

Mrs. Sophia A. Hawthorne,
Care of Dr. N. Peabody,
Boston, Mass.

TO MRS. HAWTHORNE

Salem, December 20th (Friday morning), 1844

Sweetest Phoebe,

It will be a week tomorrow since I left thee; and in all that time, I have heard nothing of thee, nor thou of me. Nevertheless, I am not anxious, because I know thou wouldst write to me at once, were anything amiss. But truly my heart is not a little hungry and thirsty for thee; so, of my own accord, or rather of my own necessity, I sit down to write thee a word or two. First of all, I love thee. Also, I love our little Una—and, I think, with a much more adequate comprehension of her loveliness, than before we left Concord. She is partly worthy of being thy daughter;—if not wholly to, it must be her father's fault.

Mine own, I know not what to say to thee. I feel now as when we clasp one another in our arms, and are silent.

Our mother and sisters were rejoiced to see me, and not altogether surprised; for they seem to 121 have had a kind of presentiment of my return. Mother had wished Louisa to write for us both to come back; but I think it would not be wise to bring Una here again, till warm weather. I am not without apprehensions that she will have grown too tender to bear the atmosphere of our cold and windy old Abbey in Concord, after becoming acclimated to the milder temperature of thy father's house. However, we will trust to Providence, and likewise to a good fire in our guest-chamber. Thou wilt write to me when all things are propitious for our return. They wish me to stay here till after Christmas;—which I think is next Wednesday—but I care little about festivals. My only festival is when I have thee. But I suppose we shall not get home before the last of next week;—it will not do to delay our return much longer than that, else we shall be said to have run away from our creditors.

If I had not known it before, I should have been taught by this long separation, that the only real life is to be with thee—to be thy husband—thy intimatest, thy lovingest, thy belovedest—and to share all things, good or evil, with thee. The days and weeks that I have spent away from thee are unsubstantial—there is nothing in them—and yet they have done me good, in making me more 122 conscious of this truth. Now that I stand a little apart from our Concord life, the troubles and incommodities look slighter—our happiness more vast and inestimable. I trust Heaven will not permit us to be greatly pinched by poverty, during the remainder of our stay there. It would be a pity to have our recollection of this first home darkened by such associations,—the home where our love first assumed human life in the form of our darling child.

I hear nothing yet from O'Sullivan—nor from Bridge. I am afraid the latter gentleman must be ill; else, methinks, he would certainly have written; for he has always been a punctual correspondent, when there was anything to write about.

Ownest Dove, I think I shall not go back to Hillard's. I shall be ready to go back to Concord whenever thou art; but, not having the opportunity to consult thee, I now propose that we settle our return for Saturday, a week from tomorrow. Should anything prevent thee from going then (for instance, the want of a girl) I may go and pay our debts, as far as in my power, and then return. But this need not be anticipated. There is no absolute necessity—(except in our hearts, which cannot endure to be away from one another much longer)—for our being at home before the 123 first of January; but if all things are convenient, we will not delay longer than Saturday. Oh, what sweet, sweet times we will have.

Give Una a kiss, and her father's blessing. She is very famous here in Salem.

Mrs. Sophia A. Hawthorne,
Care of Dr. N. Peabody,
Boston, Mass.

TO MRS. HAWTHORNE

Salem, April 14th (Sunday), 1844

Ownest Phoebe,

Thy letter reached me yesterday forenoon, and made me truly happy—happier than I can tell. I do not think that I am the more conscious of the baby, by standing aloof from her. She has not yet sufficiently realised herself in my soul; it seems like a dream, therefore, which needs such assurances as thy letter, to convince me that it is more than a dream. Well; I cannot write about her—nor about thee, belovedest, for whom I have at this moment an unutterable yearning. Methinks my hand was never so out of keeping with my heart.

I called at the book room in Boston, and saw there thy mother, thy brother Nat, and Elizabeth!!—besides two or three ladies. It was the most awkward place in the world to talk about Una and other kindred subjects; so I made my escape as soon as possible, promising to return to 125 dine if convenient, and resolving that it should be as inconvenient as possible. I wish thy mother could be so inhospitable as never to ask me—but at all events, I need never go, except when thou art there. I went to George Hillard's office, and he spoke with unmitigable resolution of the necessity of my going to dine with Longfellow before returning to Concord; but I have an almost miraculous power of escaping from necessities of this kind. Destiny itself has often been worsted in the attempt to get me out to dinner. Possibly, however, I may go. Afterwards I called on Colonel Hall, who held me long in talk about politics and other sweetmeats. Here, likewise, I refused one or two invitations to dinner. Then I stept into a book-auction, not to buy, but merely to observe; and after a few moments, who should come in, with a smile as sweet as sugar (though savoring rather of molasses) but, to my horror and petrifaction, Mr. Watterson! I anticipated a great deal of bore and botheration; but, through Heaven's mercy, he merely spoke a few words, and then left me. This is so unlike his deportment in times past, that I suspect the Celestial Railroad must have given him a pique; and if so, I shall feel as if Providence had sufficiently rewarded me for that pious labor. 126

In the course of the forenoon, I encountered Mr. Howes in the street. He looked most exceedingly depressed, and pressing my hand with peculiar emphasis, said that he was in great affliction, having just had news of his son George's death in Cuba. He seemed encompassed and overwhelmed by the misfortune, and walked the street as in a heavy cloud of his own grief, forth from which he extended his hand to meet my grasp. I expressed my sympathy, which I told him I was now the more capable of feeling in a father's suffering, as being myself the father of a little girl—and, indeed, the being a parent does give one the freedom of a wider range of sorrow as well as happiness. He again pressed my hand, and left me.

Well, dove, when I got to Salem, there was great joy, as you may suppose. Our mother and sisters take as much interest in little Una as can possibly be desired. They think the lock of hair very beautiful, and deny that it has the faintest tinge of red. Mother hinted an apprehension that poor baby would be spoilt—whereupon I irreverently observed, that having spoilt her own three children, it was natural for her to suppose that all other parents would do the same; when she knocked me into a cocked 127 hat, by averring that it was impossible to spoil such children as Elizabeth and me, because she had never been able to do anything with us. This I believe to be very true. There was too much gentleness in her nature for such a task. She remonstrates, by the by, against Una's being carried about in anybody's arms, and says that it will soon be impossible to keep her quiet in any other way. This was the case with Elizabeth; and mother never allowed her other children to become habituated to it.

I could scarcely convince them that Una has begun to smile so soon. It surprised even mother; though her own children appear to have been bright specimens of babyhood. Elizabeth could walk and talk at nine months old. I do not understand that thy husband was quite such a miracle of precocity, but should think it not improbable, inasmuch as precocious boys are said to make stupid men.

Ownest wife, I long so much to get back to thee, that it is a mockery to try to say how much. Yet I think I shall be benefitted by the absence, though it be truly an unpalatable medicine. I hope thy father will be able to stay till Friday. It is just possible, if I go out to see Longfellow, that 128 I may not come till Saturday night; but this will depend partly on what day the steamer comes. I shall consult thy mother about the necessity of thy father's presence in Boston earlier than that.

Mrs. Sophia A. Hawthorne,
Concord, Massachusetts.

TO MRS. HAWTHORNE

Concord, May 27th, 1844

Dearest Phoebe,

I cannot let the day pass without speaking a little word to thee, to tell thee how strange the old Abbey seems without thy presence, and how strange this life, when thou art away. Nevertheless, I truly rejoice in thy absence, as hoping it will do good to thy dearest brain, which has been over-wrought, as well as thy physical frame. And how does our belovedest little Una? whom I love more than I ever told thee, though not more than thou knowest—for is she not thine and mine, the symbol of the one true union in the world, and of our love in Paradise.

Dearest, my cook does his office admirably. He prepared what I must acknowledge to be the best dish of fried fish and potatoes for dinner to-day, that I ever tasted in this house. I scarcely recognized the fish of our own river. I make him get all the dinners while I confine myself to the much 130 lighter labors of breakfast and tea. He also takes his turn at washing the dishes. Ellery Channing came to see me this morning, and was very gracious and sociable; and we went a fishing together. He says his little girl weighed seven pounds at her birth, and is doing very well. Miss Prescott is now there.

We had a very pleasant dinner at Longfellow's; and I liked Mrs. Longlady (as thou naughtily nicknamest her) quite much. The dinner was late, and we sate long; so that Conolly and I did not get here till half-past nine o'clock—and truly the old house seemed somewhat dark and desolate. The next morning came George Prescott with Una's lion, who greeted me very affectionately, but whined and moaned as if he missed somebody who should have been here. I am not quite as strict as I should be in keeping him out of the house; but I commiserate him and myself—for are we not both of us bereaved. Still I am happy, and more quiet than when thou wast here; because I feel it to be good for thee to be there. Dearest, keep thyself at peace, and do not let persons nor things trouble thee; and let other people take all the care of Una that is possible; and do not fear to go out occasionally; and think sometimes of thy husband, who loves thee unspeakably; and because he cannot 131 tell its immensity, he may as well stop here, especially as Conolly (whom I can no more keep from smoking than I could the kitchen chimney) has just come into the study with a cigar, which might perfume this letter, and make thee think it came from thy husband's own enormity.

I love thee. I love thee.

Mrs. Sophia A. Hawthorne,
Care of Dr. N. Peabody,
Boston, Massachusetts.

TO MRS. HAWTHORNE

Concord, May 29th, 1844

Ownest Wife,

Conolly is leaving me, to my unspeakable relief; for he has had a bad cold, which caused him to be much more troublesome, and less amusing, than might otherwise have been the case. Thy husband is in perfect health; and as happy in the prospect of being alone, as he would be in anything, except to be reunited to thee. I suppose I must invite Mr. Farley to come by-and-by; but not quite yet—Oh, not quite yet—it is so sweet to be alone. I want to draw a little free breath. Ah, why canst not thou be with me here—and no Mary—no nobody else! But our little Una! Should not she be of the party? Yes; we have linked a third spirit forever to our own; and there is no existing without her.

Dearest Phoebe, I do trust thou art well and at ease. Thou absolutely knowest not how I love thee. God bless thee, mine ownest—God bless 133 our daughter—God bless thy husband—God bless us altogether, and the whole world too.

I write in the greatest hurry.

THINE OWNEST
HUSBAND.

Have no apprehensions on my account. I shall write to Farley at the end of the week—and till then shall bathe myself in solitude.

Mrs. Sophia A. Hawthorne,
Care of Dr. N. Peabody,
13 West-street,
Boston, Mass.

TO MRS. HAWTHORNE

Concord, May 31st, 1844

Ownest Phoebe,

Thy two dearest letters have been received, and gave me infinite comfort. Oh, keep thyself quiet, best wife, and do not think of coming home till thou art quite cured, even though Una should grow to be quite a large girl in the interim. As for me, I get along admirably, and am at this moment superintending the corned beef, which has been on the fire, as it appears to me, ever since the beginning of time, and shows no symptom of being done before the crack of doom. Mrs. Hale says it must boil till it becomes tender; and so it shall, if I can find wood to keep the fire a-going. Meantime, I keep my station in the dining-room, and read or write as composedly as in my own study. Just now, there came a very important rap to the front door; and I threw down a smoked herring which I had begun to eat (as there is no hope of the corned beef to-day) and went to admit 135 the visitor. Who should it be but Ben, with a very peculiar and mysterious grin upon his face! He put into my hands a missive directed to "Mr. and Mrs. Hawthorne"; it contained a little hit of card signifying that "Dr. Lemuel Fuller and Miss Catherine Barrett receive their friends Thursday Eve, June 6th, at 8 o'clock." I am afraid I shall be too busy washing my dishes, to pay many visits during thy absence. This washing of dishes does seem to me the most absurd and unsatisfactory business that I ever undertook. If, when once washed, they would remain clean forever and ever, (which they ought in all reason to do, considering how much trouble it is,) there would be less occasion to grumble; but no sooner is it done, than it requires to be done again. On the whole I have come to the resolution not to use more than one dish at each meal. However, I moralise deeply on this and other matters, and have discovered that all the trouble and affliction in the world arises from the necessity of cleansing away our earthly pollutions.

I ate the last morsel of bread, yesterday, and congratulated myself on being now reduced to the fag-end of necessity. Nothing worse can happen (according to ordinary modes of thinking) than to want bread; but, like most afflictions, it is worse 136 in prospect than reality. I found one cracker in the tureen, and exulted over it as if it had been so much gold. However, I have sent a petition to Mrs. Prescott, stating my destitute condition, and imploring her succor; and till it arrives, I shall keep myself alive on smoked herrings and apples, together with part of a pint of milk, which I share with Leo. He is my great trouble now, though an excellent companion too. But it is not easy to find food for him, unless I give him what is fit for Christians—though, for that matter, he appears to be as good a Christian as most laymen, or even as some of the clergy. I fried some pouts and eels, yesterday, on purpose for him; for he does not like raw fish. They were very good; but I should hardly have taken the trouble on my own account.

George Prescott has just come to say, that Mrs. Prescott has no bread at present, and is gone away this afternoon, but that she will send me some tomorrow. I mean to have a regular supply from the same source—which thou shalt repay after thy return.

I go to bed at dusk, now-a-days, out of a tender consideration for the oil-can, which does not possess the peculiar virtues of the Widow Cruse's. [sic] Oh, dear little wife! Dost thou even 137 think of me? I think of thee continually, and of our darling Una, and long to see both thee and her, yet not with an impatient and importunate longing. I am too sure of my treasures not to be able to bear a little separation of them, when it is for thine own good. Thou needest be under no uneasiness for my sake. Everything goes on well, and I enjoy my solitude, next to thy society. I suppose I shall write to Mr. Farley tomorrow, but it would content me well to be quite alone till thy return. Thou canst not imagine how much the presence of Leo relieves the feeling of perfect loneliness. He insists upon being in the room with me all the time, (except at night, when he sleeps in the shed) and I do not find myself severe enough to drive him out. He accompanies me, likewise, on all my walks, to the village and elsewhere; and, in short, keeps at my heels all the time, except when I go down cellar. Then he stands at the head of the stairs and howls, as if he never expected to see me again. He is evidently impressed with the present solitude of our old Abbey, both on his own account and mine, and feels that he may assume a greater degree of intimacy than would be otherwise allowable. He will easily be brought within the old regulations, after thy return. 138

Ownest, I have written to-day, because I thought thou wouldst be anxious to know what sort of a life I lead, now that my guest has departed. Thou wilt see that I am fit to be trusted in my own keeping. No ghost has haunted me, and no living thing has harmed me. God bless thee and our little Una. I say to myself, when I feel lonely, "I am a husband!—I am a father!"—and it makes me so happy!.

P.S.—Three o'clock.—The beef is done!!!

Mrs. Sophia A. Hawthorne,
Care of Dr. N. Peabody,
Boston, Massachusetts

TO MRS. HAWTHORNE

Concord, June 2[d], 1844. 12 o'clock

Mine ownest,

Thy letter was brought this morning by one of the Fullers—which, I know not—but it was the young man who called on us last winter; and he promises to call and take this. Sweetest, if it troubles thee to write, thou must not make the attempt. Perhaps it is not good for thy head; and thy mother can just say a word or two, to let me know that all is going on well. Oh, keep thyself quiet, dearest wife, and let not thy brain be whirled round in the vortex of thy present whereabout; else I must have thee back again as soon as possible. But if it be for thy good, I can spare thee at least a month longer; indeed, thou must not come till the Doctor has both found out thy disorder and cured it.

Everything goes on well with thy husband. Thou knowest, at the time of writing my last letter, 140 I was without bread. Well, just at supper time came Mrs. Brown with a large covered dish, which proved to contain a quantity of special good slap jacks, piping hot, prepared, I suppose, by the fair hands of Miss Martha or Miss Abby; for Mrs. Prescott was not at home. They served me both for supper and breakfast; and I thanked Providence and the young ladies, and compared myself to the prophet fed by ravens—though the simile does rather more than justice to myself, and not enough to the generous donors of the slap jacks. The next morning, Mrs. Prescott herself brought two big loaves of bread, which will last me a week, unless I have some guests to provide for. I have likewise found a hoard of crackers in one of the covered dishes; so that the old castle is sufficiently provisioned to stand a long siege. The cornbeef is exquisitely done, and as tender as a young lady's heart, all owing to my skilful cookery; for I consulted Mrs. Hale at every step; and precisely followed her directions. To say the truth, I look upon it as such a masterpiece in its way, that it seems irreverential to eat it; so perhaps thou wilt find it almost entire at thy return. Things on which so much thought and labor are bestowed should surely be immortal.

Ellery Channing intends to make a tour presently. 141 Wm. Fuller says he is at variance with Miss Prescott—or at least is uncomfortable in the house with her. What a gump! I have had some idea of inviting him to stay here till thy return; but really, on better consideration, the experiment would be too hazardous. If he cannot keep from quarrelling with his wife's nurse, he would surely quarrel with me, alone in an empty house; and perhaps the result might be a permanent breach. On the whole, he is but little better than an idiot. He should have been whipt often and soundly in his boyhood; and as he escaped such wholesome discipline then, it might be well to bestow it now. But somebody else may take him in hand; it is none of my business.

Leo and I attended divine services, this morning, in a temple not made with hands. We went to the farthest extremity of Peter's path, and there lay together under an oak, on the verge of the broad meadow. Dearest Phoebe, thou shouldst have been there. Thy head would have been quite restored by the delicious air, which was too good and pure for anybody but thee to breathe. Shouldst thou not walk out, every day, round the common, at least, if not further? Thou must not fear to leave Una occasionally. I shall not love her, if she imprisons thee when thy health 142 requires thee to be abroad. Do not people offer to take thee to ride?

I doubt whether Mr. Bradford could be comfortable here, unless there were womankind in the house to keep it in better order than it suits my convenience to do. A man of his nice conscience would be shocked, I suppose, if the whole house were not swept, every day, from top to bottom, or if the dishes of several meals were suffered to accumulate, in order to save trouble by a general cleansing. Now such enormities do not at all disturb my composure. Besides, I find myself such good company, and the hours flit so rapidly away, that I have no time to bestow on anybody else. Talk is but a waste of time. When I cannot be with thee, mine ownest—my true life—then let me be alone. I wrote to Mr. Farley, yesterday; and am sorry for it, since I received thy letter. But I presume there is no prospect of his coming; and should he do so, I shall not hesitate to advise him to go away, if our mode of life here should seem unsuitable to his condition.

Darlingest wife, when thou writest next, tell me if thou canst see the termination of thy absence; but do not think it in the least necessary to hurry on my account. I find I have shirts enough for a fortnight or three weeks longer; and 143 can get somebody to wash them, at the end of that time. Do not hurry thyself—do not be uneasy. I had rather come and see thee in Boston, than that thou shouldst return too soon.

Give my blessing to our daughter.

THY LOVINGEST
HUSBAND.

Mrs. Sophia A. Hawthorne,
Care of Dr. N. Peabody,
13 West-street,
Boston.

By Mr. Fuller.

TO MRS. HAWTHORNE

Concord, June 6th, 1844

Mine ownest, ownest love, dost thou not want to hear from thy husband? There is no telling nor thinking how much I love thee; so we will leave all that matter without another word. Dearest, Mr. Farley arrived yesterday, and appeared to be in most excellent health, and as happy as the sunshine. Almost the first thing he did was to wash the dishes; and he is really indefatigable in the kitchen; so that thy husband is quite a gentleman of leisure. Previous to his coming, I had kindled no fire for four entire days, and had lived all that time on the corned beef—except one day, when Ellery and I went down the river on a fishing excursion. Yesterday we boiled some lamb, which we shall have cold for dinner to-day. This morning, Mr. Farley fried a sumptuous dish of eels for breakfast, and he avows his determination to make me look fat before thy return. Mrs. Prescott continues to be the instrument 145 of Providence, and yesterday sent us a very nice plum-pudding. Thou seest, therefore, that domestic matters are going on admirably. I have told Mr. Farley that I shall be engaged in the forenoons, and he is to arrange his own occupations and amusements during that time. Thus, as everything is so comfortably regulated, thou canst stay in Boston without the slightest solicitude about my welfare, as long as there is any object in being near Dr. Wesselhoeft. But how our hearts will rush together, when we meet again! Oh, how I love thee!

Not much has happened of late. Leo, I regret to say, has fallen under suspicion of a very grave crime—nothing less than murder—a fowl crime it may well be called—for it is the slaughter of one of Mr. Hayward's hens. He has been seen to chase the hens, several times, and the other day one of them was found dead. Possibly he may be innocent; and as there is nothing but circumstantial evidence, it must be left with his own conscience. Meantime, Mr. Hayward or somebody else seems to have given him such a whipping, that he is absolutely stiff, and walks about like a rheumatic old gentleman. I am afraid, too, that he is an incorrigible thief. Ellery Channing says he saw him coming up the avenue with a whole 146 calf's head in his mouth. How he came by it, is best known to Leo himself. If he were a dog of fair character, it would be no more than charity to conclude that he had either bought it or had it given to him; but, with the other charges against him, it inclines me to great distrust of his moral principles. Be that as it may, he managed his stock of provisions very thriftily—burying it in the earth, and eating a portion of it whenever he felt an appetite. If he insists upon living by highway robbery, dost thou not think it would be well to make him share his booty with us? Our butcher's bill might thus be considerably lessened.

Miss Barret came a day or two ago to enquire whether I thought my wife would be willing to lend our astral lamp for the great occasion of this evening. Thou seest, she has a very proper idea of the authority of the wife, and cannot imagine that I should venture to lend any article without reference to thy wishes. As she pledged herself, if there were any damages, to "make it good," I took the liberty to put the lamp into her hands. Thou knowest its trick of going out in the middle of the evening; and it will be a truly laughable and melancholy mishap, if it should suddenly leave them in darkness, at the most critical moment. Methinks it would be no favorable omen for the prosperity of the marriage. Miss Catherine 147 regrets very much that thou art not to be here, this evening. I wonder thou dost not come on purpose. By the by, it was not our old broken astral lamp, but the solar lamp that I lent her.

Ownest wife, am I really a father?—the father of thy child! Sometimes the thought comes to me with such a mighty wonder that I cannot take it in. I love our little Una a great deal better than when I saw her last; and all the love that grows within me for her, is so much added to the infinite store of my love for thee. Ah, dost thou think of me?—dost thou yearn for me?—does thy breast heave and thy heart quake with love for thy husband?—... (portion of letter missing) I can hardly breathe for loving thee so much.

Dearest, Mr. Farley is to carry this letter to the Post-Office this morning, and perhaps he will find a line or two from thee. If so, I shall be happy; and if not, then too I shall be glad that thou hast not tasked thy dearest little head to do any pen-work.

Mrs. Sophia A. Hawthorne,
Care of Dr. N. Peabody,
Boston, Mass.

TO MRS. HAWTHORNE

Concord, June 10th, 1844

Only Belovedest,

Thy letter came yesterday; and I suppose thou didst get mine about the same time. Dearest, I take it for granted that thou hast concluded to await the arrival of the money from O'Sullivan; so that I shall not expect thee till Friday or Saturday. I think it is an excellent plan to have thy mother come with thee; so pray ask her immediately, if thou hast not done it already. I shall not be able to send away Mr. Farley before thou comest; but he will go on Monday.

Mr. Farley is in perfect health, and absolutely in the seventh Heaven; and he talks, and talks, and talks, and talks; and I listen, and listen, and listen, with a patience for which (in spite of all my sins) I firmly expect to be admitted to the mansions of the blessed. And there is really a contentment in being able to make the poor, world-worn, hopeless, half-crazy man so entirely 149 comfortable as he seems to be here. He is an admirable cook. We had some roast veal and a baked rice pudding on Sunday—really a fine dinner, and cooked in better style than Mary can equal; and George Curtis came to dine with us. Like all male cooks, he is rather expensive, and has a tendency to the consumption of eggs in his various concoctions, which thou wouldst be apt to oppose. However, we consume so much fish of our own catching, that there is no great violation of economy upon the whole. I have had my dreams of splendor, but never expected to arrive at the dignity of keeping a man-cook. At first, we had three meals a day, but now only two.

We dined at Mr. Emerson's the other day, in company with Mr. Hedge. Mr. Bradford has been to see us two or three times. And, speaking of him, do thou be most careful never to say a word in depreciation of Sarah Stearns, in his presence. Both of us (horrible to say!) have fallen into this misfortune, on former occasions. Mr. Farley has given me most unlooked for intelligence in regard to him and her. He looks thinner than ever—judge, then, how thin he must be—his face is so thin, and his nose is so sharp, that he might make a pen with it; and I wish he would make me a better one than I am now writing with. 150 He is particularly melancholy, and last Saturday, when we were alone on the river together, seemed half-inclined to tell me the why and wherefore. But I desire no such secrets. Keep this to thy little self.

I love thee, I love thee! Thou lovest me, thou lovest me! Oh, I shiver again to think how much I love thee—how much we love, and that thou art soon, soon, coming back to thine own home—to thine ownest husband; and with our beloved baby in thine arms. Shall I know little Una, dost thou think?

Now good bye, sweetest wife. It will be no more than decent for me to go down and offer my assistance to Mr. Farley in some of the minor preparations of dinner. Thy mother must put her skill in exercise; else he will find a sad falling-off in our living, after thy return. I shall look for thee partly on Friday, but shall not be disappointed if thou comest not till Saturday. God bless thee, thou belovedest.

THINE OWN HUSBAND.

Mrs. Sophia A. Hawthorne,
Care of Dr. N. Peabody,
Boston, Mass.

TO MRS. HAWTHORNE

Boston, May 23[d], 1845

Ownest Dearest,

I write this little note in order to warn thee in due season that I shall not be at home till Monday. Hillard has made an engagement for me with Longfellow for Sunday; so that, without disappointing both of those worthies exceedingly, I cannot come away sooner. Belovedest, I love thee a million times as much every hour that I stay away from thee; and my heart swells toward thee like a mighty flood. Also, I have a yearning for our little Una; and whenever I go, and with whomsoever I am talking, the thought of thee and her is ever present with me. God bless thee! What a happy home we have. That is the knowledge that I gain by staying away from thee. 152

I saw thy mother this forenoon. She told me that Elizabeth had gone to Concord this morning.

Remember me to "Our Boarder."

In utmost haste,
THINE OWNEST
HUSBAND.

Mrs. Sophia A. Hawthorne,
Concord, Mass.

TO MRS. HAWTHORNE

Salem, August 25th, 1845

Dearest Phoebe Hawthorne,

Already an age has elapsed since I parted from thee, mine own life; although, according to human measurement, it is but about twenty-seven hours. How I love thee, wife of my bosom! There is no telling; so judge it by what is in thine own deepest and widest little heart.

Sweetest, what became of that letter? Whose fault was it, that it was left behind? I was almost afraid to present myself before thy mother without it. Nevertheless, the Count and I made it our first business to call at 13 West-street, where we found Madame Peabody (I will call her so to please my Dove) in the book room alone. She seemed quite as well as usual, and regretted, I believe, that she had not gone to Concord—and so did thy husband; but thou needest not say so to the good old gentleman who sits looking at the outside of this letter, while thou art reading the 154 inside. I gave her all the information I could about thy condition—being somewhat restrained, however, by the presence of O'Sullivan.

Taking leave of thy mother, I went with the Count to Mr. Bancroft's door, and then parted with him, with some partial expectation of meeting him again at dinner. Then I looked in at the Athenaeum reading-room, and next went to George Hillard's office. Who should I find here but Longfellow, and with him Mr. Green, the Roman consul, whom, as thou knowest, it was Bridge's plan to eject from office for thy husband's benefit. He has returned to this country on a visit. Never didst thou see such an insignificant looking personage (or person rather;) and it surprised me so much the more, for I had formed a high idea of his intellectual incarnation from a bust by Crawford, at Longfellow's rooms. Longfellow himself seems to have bloomed forth and found solidity and substance since his marriage;—never did I behold a man of happier aspect; although I know one of happier fortunes incomparably. But Longfellow appears perfectly satisfied, and to be no more conscious of any earthly or spiritual trouble than a sunflower is—of which lovely blossom he, I know not why, reminded me. Hillard looked better than I have 155 ever before seen him, and was in high spirits on account of the success of his oration. It seems to have had truly triumphant success—superior to that of any Phi Beta Kappa oration ever delivered. It gladdened me most to see this melancholy shadow of a man for once bathed and even pervaded with a sunshine; and I must doubt whether any literary success of my own ever gave me so much pleasure. Outward triumphs are necessary to him; to thy husband they are anything but essential.

From Hillard's I went to see Colonel Hall, and had a talk about politics and official matters; and the good Colonel invited me to dinner; and I concluded to accept, inasmuch as, by dining with the Count, I should have been forced to encounter Brownson—from whom the Lord deliver us. These are the main incidents of the day; but I did not leave Boston till half past five, by which time I was quite wearied with the clatter and confusion of the city, so unlike our quiet brooding life at home. Oh, dear little Dove, thou shouldst have been with me; and then all the quiet would have been with me likewise.

Great was the surprise and joy of Louisa when she found me at the door. I found them all pretty well; but our poor mother seems to have 156 grown older and thinner since I saw her at last. They all inquired for thee with loving kindness. Louisa intended to come and visit us in about a week; and I shall not thwart her purpose, if it still continue. She thinks she may be ready in a week from to-day. And, dearest little wife, I fear that thy husband will have to defer his return to thy blessed arms till the same day. Longfellow wants me to dine with him on Friday; and my mother will not be content to give me up before Thursday; and indeed it is not altogether unreasonable that she should have me this long; because she will not see me again.

But, sweetest Phoebe, thou knowest not how I yearn for thee. Never hadst thou such love, as now. Oh, dearest wife, take utmost care of thyself; for if any harm should come to thee during my absence, I should always impute blame to myself. Do watch over my Dove, now that I am away. And should my presence be needful before Saturday, I will fly to thee at a moment's warning. If all continue well, I shall proceed to Boston on Thursday, visit Longfellow on Friday, and come home (Oh, happiest thought!) on Saturday night, with Louisa, if she finds it possible to come. If anything should detain her, it will be our mother's health. God bless thee. Amen. 157

Afternoon.—What a scrawl is the foregoing! I wrote fast because I loved fervently. I shall write once more before my return. Take care of thy dearest little self and do not get weary.

THY BEST OF
HUSBANDS.

Mrs. Nathaniel Hawthorne,
Concord, Massachusetts.

TO MRS. HAWTHORNE

Salem, Novr. 10th, 1845

Ownest,

It was revealed to me that thou didst write on Saturday, and so, at nightfall, I went to the Post-Office, but found no letter. This morning, it has arrived, with the postmark of to-day. It gladdens me to hear of Una's joy, and of thy being with people whom thou knowest well, and who know thee well, and with whom thou canst have real intercourse and sympathy. As for us in Castle Dismal, we miss thee greatly, all of us, and dwell in a deeper shadow for lack of thee, and that streak of living sunshine with which thou hast illuminated the earth. Whom do I mean by this brilliant simile? Can it be that little redheaded personage? Louisa complains of the silence of the house; and not all their innumerable cats avail to comfort them in the least. Thy husband thinks of thee when he ought to be scribbling nonsense—and very empty and worthless is his 159 daily life, without thee. Nevertheless, if thou art at ease, do not come home in less than a week. I feel as if it were good for thee to be there, and good for Una too. Louisa told me, yesterday, with some alarm in her manner, that Dr. Moss (thy medical friend) says that the illness from vaccination does not come on, or does not reach its crisis, till the ninth day. Can this be so? And will it be necessary to wait so long? That would postpone thy return till the middle of next week—a term to which I cannot yet reconcile myself.

I read Una's note, addressed to "Madame Hawthorne," then sealed it up and threw it downstairs. Doubtless, they find it a most interesting communication; and I feel a little shamefaced about meeting them.

I hear nothing from Washington as yet; nor, indeed, is it yet time to expect any definite intelligence. Meanwhile Pike and thy friend David are planning to buy us an estate, and build a house, and have even gone so far as to mark out the ground-plot of the house, in chalk, on David's hearth. I fear it will prove a castle in the air; and yet, a moderate smile of Providence would cause it to spring out of the earth, on that beautiful hillside, like a flower in the summer time. With a cottage of our own, and the surveyorship, 160 how happy we might be!—happier than in Concord, on many accounts. The Surveyorship I think we shall have; but the cottage implies an extra thousand or fifteen hundred dollars.

I have heard of Mr. Atherton's being in Boston since thy departure;—whether Mrs. Atherton is with him I know not. Governor Fairfield, I understand, starts for Washington to-day.

God bless thee, dearest!—and blessed be our daughter, whom I love next to thee! Again, if thou feelest it good for thee, on any account, to stay longer in Boston, do not hasten home;—but whenever thou comest, my heart will open to take thee in.

THY   LOVINGEST HUSBAND.

TO MRS. HAWTHORNE

Castle Dismal, Novr. 13th, 1845

Intimatest Friend,

I cannot settle down to work this forenoon, or do anything but write to thee—nor even that, I fear, with any good effect; for I am just as much dissatisfied with this mode of intercourse as always hitherto. It is a wretched mockery. But then it *is* a semblance of communication, and, thus far, better than nothing.

I got thy letter of Tuesday the same evening, while it was still warm out of thy heart; and it seemed to fill the air round about me with Nona's prattle. I do love her—that is the truth,—and almost feel it a pity to lose a single day of her development;—only thou wilt tell me, by letter or by mouth, all the pretty things that she says or does, and more over find a beauty in them which would escape my grosser perception. Thus, on the whole, I shall be a gainer by our occasional separations. Thee I miss, and without any recompense. 162 I marvel how it is that some husbands spend years and years away from their wives, and then come home with perhaps a bag or two of gold, earned by the sacrifice of all that life. Even poverty is better—and in saying that, thou knowest how much I say.

Nothing has happened here since I wrote thee last. I suspect the intelligence of thy meditated baby is very pleasant to the grandmother and aunts; for Louisa met me at dinner, that day, with unusual cheerfulness, and observed that Thanksgiving was at hand, and that we must think of preparing. [As] for me, I already love the future little personage; and yet, somehow or other, I feel a jealousy of him or her, on Una's account, and should not choose to have the new baby better than the old one. So take care what thou dost, Phoebe Hawthorne! And now I think of it, do not thou venture into that tremendous press and squeeze, which always takes place on landing from the ferry-boat at the East Boston depot. Thou art not to be trusted in such a tumult; it will be far better to wait behind, and compel the conductor to find thee a seat. There is always the densest squeeze on Saturdays.

But I shall not expect thee back on Saturday. According to Dr. Wesselhoeft's dictum, and supposing 163 the vaccination to have taken, that will be precisely the critical day;—if Dr. Moss be correct, the crisis comes on Monday. In either case, I hope thou wilt wait a little. There is the greatest satisfaction to me in thinking how comfortably situated thou art, with thy sister at thy elbow, and thy mother at arms' length, and thy Aesculapius within a five minutes' summons. If I (and thou too, thou lovingest one) could endure it, I should be glad that thou mightest spend the winter there; but that is too heart-chilling to think of—so thou must even come back, in a few days more, to old Castle Dismal! But I shall never feel at home here with thee. I went, the other afternoon, to look at the hill where Pike and the Chancellor have built a castle in the air for our reception. Thou hast no idea what capacities it has.

(Portion of letter missing) 164

TO MRS. HAWTHORNE

Salem, Jany. 19th, 1846.—
Tuesday

Ownest Phoebe,

The shoe arrived last evening; but on what evidence thou dost so confidently accuse me of putting it into the trunk, I cannot imagine. Thou positively didst put it there thyself. I saw thee!

Dearest, if any money comes from New York by to-day's mail, I will come to Boston on Thursday morning, to escort thee home. Otherwise, I really do not think I ought. Heaven knows, I desire it; but as it is not necessary for thy safety, and as we are so miserably poor, methinks the dollar should be reserved for indispensables. I did hope the New York money would have come to hand before now. Providence must take our matters in hand very speedily.

I hope, Phoebe, thou hast not engaged to pay Winifred's passage, either to or from Boston. She told Mrs. Dromedary that she should not have 165 gone with thee, only that her passage would be paid. She has a cousin living at the Essex House in this city; and the Dromedary thinks she is partly engaged to go there herself. This is the secret of her willingness to remain in Salem. Dotish as she appeared, she has wit enough to be fair and false, like all her countryfolk. It will be well to investigate this matter before thou returnest; and, if she really means to leave us, perhaps thou hadst better engage a new girl in Boston forthwith.

Poor little Una's back—my heart bleeds for it. Do not come back till it is well, nor till thou thyself hast undergone thorough repairs, even though thou shouldst be compelled to hire a lodging.

Ownest, be careful not to slip down. Thou art prudent in behalf of other people, but hast little caution on thine own account. In going to the cars do not get entangled in that great rush of people who throng out of the ferry-boat. Remain behind, and Heaven will find thee a seat. Would thou wast safe home again, eating thy potatoes, and glancing sideways at me with thy look of patient resignation. Never did I miss thee so much as during this separation. But for the idea of thee, my existence would be as cold and wintry as the weather is now, and with a cloudy gloom 166 besides, instead of the dazzling sunshine. I was driven to play cards with Louisa, last evening!

God bless thee! I have nothing more to say, that can be said.

THINE OWNEST
HUSBAND.

Mrs. Sophia A. Hawthorne,
Care of Dr. N. Peabody,
Boston, Massachusetts.

TO MRS. HAWTHORNE

Salem, April 24th, 1846.—6 P.M.

Ownest dearest,

I have this moment received the packet and thy letter, and cannot tolerate that thou shouldst not have a word from thy husband tomorrow morning. Truly, Castle Dismal has seemed darker than ever, since I returned to it;—and not only to me, but to its other inmates. Louisa spoke of the awful stillness of the house, and said she could not bear to give Una's old shoes to that little Lines child, and was going to keep them herself. I rejoiced her much, by telling her of Una's home-sickness.

Fees were tolerably good, yesterday and to-day; and I doubt we shall have enough to live on, during thy continuance in Boston—for which let us be thankful.

Bridge came to see me this afternoon, and says Mary Pray has consented to come to thee; and by this time, I hope, thou hast her. Thou canst not 168 think what a peace I enjoy in the consideration that thou art within reach of Dr. Wesselhoeft. It is by my feelings as to thee and Una, more than on my own account, that I find I am a true believer in homeopathy.

Ownest, I love thee. I love little Una dearly too. Tell her so, and show her the place, and give her a kiss for me.

THINE   OWNEST HUSBAND.

Mrs. Sophia A. Hawthorne,
Care of Dr. N. Peabody,
Boston, Massachusetts.

TO MRS. HAWTHORNE

[Salem, March 15th, 1847]

Ownest Phoebe,

Above is the note. I will not say how much beyond all money I feel indebted to Mr. Shaw for his kindness. It relieves my spirits from a great burthen, and now I feel calm and very happy.

I love thee infinitely, and need thee constantly. I long to hear Una's voice. I find that I even love Bundlebreech!!!

Ellery and I have a very pleasant time, and take immense walks every afternoon, and sit up talking till midnight. He eats like an Anaconda. Thou didst never see such an appetite.

Thou dost not tell me when thou wilt turn thy face homeward. Shouldst thou stay till next week, I will come and escort thee home. Ellery, I suppose, will go as soon as Saturday. (I shall 170 need some money to come with. Couldst thou send me ten dollars?) In haste, in depths of love.

Mrs. Sophia A. Hawthorne,
Care of Dr. N. Peabody,
Boston, Massachusetts.

TO MRS. HAWTHORNE

Salem, March 20th, 1847.—
Saturday

Ownest Wife,

Thy letter of Thursday did not reach me till this morning. Ellery goes to-day—much to my satisfaction, though we have had a good time. Thou dost not know how much I long to see thee and our children. I never felt anything like it before—it is too much to write about.

I do not think I can come on Monday before 10 ½, arriving in Boston at about 11. It is no matter about the session at Johnson's; and if thou choosest to give him notice, so be it.

Now that the days are so long, would it not do to leave Boston, on our return, at ½ past 4?

Kiss Una for me—likewise Bundlebreech.

P.S. Of course, my coming on Monday must be contingent on reasonably pleasant weather. 172

I shall probably go to Johnson's immediately after my arrival—before coming to West-street. I hope he will be otherwise engaged.

Mrs. Sophia A. Hawthorne,
Care of Dr. N. Peabody,
Boston, Massachusetts

TO MRS. HAWTHORNE

Salem, July 13th, 1847

Ownest Phoebe,

Greatly needed by me were thy two letters; for thou hadst never before been away from me so long without writing. And thou art still busy, every moment! I was in hopes thou wouldst have a little quiet now, with Dora to take care of the children;—but that seems fated never more to be thine. As for me, I sink down into bottomless depths of quiet:—never was such a quiet life as mine is, in this voiceless house. Thank God, there are echoes of voices in my heart, else I should die of this marble silence. Yet I am happy, and, dearest Phoebe, I wish that thou, likewise, couldst now and then stand apart from thy lot, in the same manner, and behold how fair it is. I think we are very happy—a truth that is not always so evident to me, until I step aside from our daily life. How I love thee!—how I love our children! Can it be that we are really parents!—that 174 two beautiful lives have gushed out of our life! I am now most sensible of the wonder, and the mystery, and the happiness.

Sweetest wife, I have nothing to tell thee. My life goes on as regularly as our kitchen clock. It has no events, and therefore can have no history.

Well; when our children—these two, and three or four more are grown up, and married off, thou wilt have a little leisure, and mayst paint that Grecian picture that used to haunt thy fancy. But then our grandchildren—Una's children, and Bundlebreech's,—will be coming upon the stage. In short, after a woman has become a mother, she may find rest in Heaven, but nowhere else.

This pen is so horrible that it impedes my thought. I cannot write any more with it. Dearest, stay as long as it is good for the children and thyself. I have great joy in thinking how good it has been for Una to have this change. When thou comest back to me, it will be as the coming of an angel, and with a cherub in each hand. Indeed, it does not require absence and distance to make an angel of thee; but the divine qualities of the children do become somewhat more apparent, by occasionally getting beyond the reach of their clamor.

I think I had better not come on Saturday; but 175 if thou wilt tell me the day of thy return, I will come in the afternoon, and escort thee back. Poor little Una! How will she bear to be caged up here again. Give her a kiss for me, and tell her I want to see her *very much.* I have been much affected by a little shoe of hers, which I found on the floor. Does Bundlebreech walk yet?.

Mrs. Sophia A. Hawthorne,
Care of Dr. N. Peabody,
Boston, Massachusetts.

TO MRS. HAWTHORNE

Salem, Oct. 7th, 1847

Ownest Phoebe,

Thy letter has just come. I knew the day would not pass over without one. Would that my love could transform this ugly east wind into the sweet south-west—then wouldst thou be full of pleasant air and sunshine. I want to be near thee, and rest thee.

Dearest, the things all arrived safe—not having suffered even the dollar's worth of damage to which the man restricted himself. The carpet shall not be put down till thou comest. There is no need of it, except to save thee the trouble. We are in hopes of getting an elderly woman (Hannah Lord, whom I think thou hast heard of) for a handmaiden, but this is not so certain as I could wish. Our mother and Louisa repugn at the idea of an Irish girl; and there are scarcely any others to be heard of. I should not wonder, after 177 all, if we had to seek one in Boston. The usual price here is $1.25. I trust we shall be provided by the time thou art ready to come; but if otherwise, Mrs. Campbell is now well, and can officiate for a few days.

Duyckinck writes me that the African Cruise has come to a second edition. It is also to be published in a cheaper style, as one of the numbers of a District School Library.

The weather is so bad that I hope thou wilt not have gone to Horn pond to-day. How different these east winds are from anything that we felt in Concord. Nevertheless, I feel relieved at having left that place of many anxieties, and believe that we shall pass a happy winter here. All that I need is to have shelter, and clothes, and daily bread, for thee and Una, without the anguish of debt pressing upon me continually;—and then I would not change places with the most fortunate person in the world. What a foolish sentence that is! As if I would change places, in our worst estate, either with man or angel.

Phoebe, I think I had better not come for thee till Monday, as the weather is so unpropitious for thy visits. If that be too soon, tell me; for thou hadst better calculate on not seeing Boston again for some months; and, that being the case, it will 178 be advisable to act as if thou wast going to make a voyage to Europe.

I find I shall love thee as thou never wast loved before. God bless our little Una. She is our daughter! What a miracle! I love mother and child so much that I can put nothing into words.

I think I shall be diligent with my pen, in this old chamber whence so many foolish stories have gone forth to the world. I have already begun to scribble something for Wiley & Putnam.

THINE OWNEST OWN
HUSBAND.

Mrs. Sophia A. Hawthorne,
Care of Dr. N. Peabody,
Boston, Mass.

TO MRS. HAWTHORNE

Surveyor's Office, *Salem*, May 5th, 1848

Ownest Phoebe,

I am altogether in favor of getting the six chairs; as to the glass, I know not what to think. In fact, I must leave all other articles to thy judgment, and shall be satisfied, whatever thou dost. We can dispense with the glass better than with anything else. I rather covet the large marble-top table; but perhaps the repairs would make it otherwise than cheap.

Una behaves (as thou wouldst affirm) like an angel. We rode out to Lynn, yesterday afternoon, and had a long walk—much to her delight. I bathed her this morning; and I believe she has not shown the slightest wilfulness or waywardness, since thy departure. We have very loving times together.

I had a great mind to come to Boston, yesterday, 180 with Una, instead of alighting at Lynn. I felt thy magnetism drawing me thither.

If thou canst get me a book or two, I shall be glad. Kiss old Bundlebreech, and ask him if he remembers me. If thou art very desirous of it, thou mayst stay till Monday—or, indeed, a week or two longer—or ten years, if thou thinkest proper. I seem already to have been solitary at least so long.

Mrs. Sophia A. Hawthorne,
Care of Dr. N. Peabody,
Boston, Mass.

TO MRS. HAWTHORNE

Surveyor's Office, [*Salem,*]
June 19th, 1848

Only Belovedest,

I received thy letter on Saturday evening, and was more refreshed by it than if it had been a draft of ice-water—a rather inapt comparison, by the way. Thou canst have no imagination how lonely our house is. The rooms seem twice as large as before—and so awfully quiet! I wish, sometime or other, thou wouldst let me take the two children and go away for a few days, and thou remain behind. Otherwise, thou canst have no idea of what it is. I really am half afraid to be alone, and feel shy about looking across the dimly moon-lighted chamber. I expend a great deal of sentiment as often as I chance to see any garment of thine, in my rambles about the house, or any of the children's playthings. And after all, there is a strange bliss in being made sensible 182 of the happiness of my customary life, by this blank interval.

Tell my little daughter Una that her dolly, since her departure, has been blooming like a rose—such an intense bloom, indeed, that I rather suspected her of making free with the brandy-bottle. On taxing her with it, however, she showed no signs of guilt or confusion; and I trust it was owing merely to the hot weather. The color has now subsided into quite a moderate tint, and she looks splendidly at a proper distance; though, on too close inspection, her skin appears rather coarse—not altogether unlike that of thy good Aunt B. She has contracted an unfortunate habit of squinting; and her mouth, I am sorry to say, is somewhat askew. I shall take her to task on these matters, and hope to produce a reformation. Should I fail, thou must take her in hand. Give Una a kiss, and tell her I love her dearly. The same to little Bundlebreech, who has probably forgot "faver" by this time.

Dora complains terribly of lonesomeness, and so does Aunty N. In short, we are pretty forlorn. Nevertheless, I have much joy in your all being in the country, and hope thou wilt stay as long as thou feelest it to be for the best. How I love the children!—how I love thee, best of 183 wives!—and how I shall make thee feel it, when thou comest home! Dost thou love me?

THINE OWNEST
HUSBAND.

Mrs. Sophia A. Hawthorne,
Newton, Mass.

TO MRS. HAWTHORNE

Dearest Phoebe, when I saw thy thick letter, last night, I could not imagine what might be its contents, unless thou hadst sent a large package of the precious roses, which I should have kissed with great reverence and devotion. Thou wast naughty not to do it. But the letter truly refreshed my heart's thirst; and Una's also were very delightful. What a queer epistle was that which she dictated! It seemed as if she were writing from Paradise to comfort me on earth.

Dearest, I long for thee as thou dost for me. My love has increased infinitely since the last time we were separated. I can hardly bear to think of thy staying away yet weeks longer. I think of thee all the time. The other night, I dreamed that I was at Newton, in a room with thee, and with several other people; and thou tookst occasion to announce, that thou hadst now ceased to be my wife, and hadst taken another husband. 185 Thou madest this intelligence known with such perfect composure and *sang froid*—not particularly addressing me, but the company generally—that it benumbed my thoughts and feelings, so that I had nothing to say. Thou wast perfectly decided, and I had only to submit without a word. But, hereupon, thy sister Elizabeth, who was likewise present, informed the company, that, in this state of affairs, having ceased to be thy husband, I of course became hers; and turning to me, very coolly inquired whether she or I should write to inform my mother of the new arrangement! How the children were to be divided, I know not. I only know that my heart suddenly broke loose, and I began to expostulate with thee in an infinite agony, in the midst of which I awoke; but the sense of unspeakable injury and outrage hung about me for a long time—and even yet it has not quite departed. Thou shouldst not behave so, when thou comest to me in dreams.

I had a letter from Bridge, yesterday, dated in the latter part of April. He seems to be having a very pleasant time with his wife; but I do not understand that she is, as the Germans say, "of good hope." In the beginning of the letter, he says that Mrs. Bridge will return to America this summer. In another part, he says that the ship 186 in which he is will probably return late in the autumn; but he rather wishes that it may [be] delayed till Spring, because Mrs. Bridge desires to spend the winter in Italy.

Oh, Phoebe, I want thee much. My bosom needs thy head upon it,—thou alone art essential. Thou art the only person in the world that ever was necessary to me. Other people have occasionally been more or less agreeable; but I think I was always more at ease alone than in anybody's company, till I knew thee. And now I am only myself when thou art within my reach. Thou art an unspeakably beloved woman. How couldst thou inflict such frozen agony upon me, in that dream! Thou shouldst have caressed me and embraced me.

But do not think, much as I want thee, that I wish thee to come as long as thou judgest it good for the children to be away, and as long as thou thinkest we can afford the expense. We have a pervading happiness, that goes on whether we are present or absent in the body. Their happiness depends upon time and place; and the difference to them between town and country must be almost that of a cage or the free air, to the birds. And then it is so much better for their health.

Hast thou remembered to ask Mrs. Mann 187 whether little Pick Mann was named out of pure gratitude and respect for the old refugee Colonel, or whether there was not a little earthly alloy—an idea of gilding an ugly name with a rich legacy?

Ownest, if I write any more, it would be only to try to express more lovings, and longings—and as they are impossible to express, I may as well close.

My only belovedest,
THY BEST BELOVED.

Mrs. Sophia A. Hawthorne,
West Newton.

TO MRS. HAWTHORNE

Salem, July 1st, 1848

Ownest, How long is it since I heard from thee—and what an eternity since thou didst go away! It seems at least as long as the whole time that we have been married. My heart calls for thee, very loudly, and thou comest not. And I want to hear our children's voices;—it would be pleasant, even, to see little Tornado in one of her tantrums. She is a noble child. Kiss her and Bundlebreech for me, and talk to them about me, lest I be entirely forgotten.

If this had been a pleasant day, I should probably have gone to New York on Custom-House business; but it being thick and dismal, I shall give up the expedition, although it would have been a very favorable opportunity. I should have been back here on Wednesday morning; and as one of the intervening days is Sunday, and 189 another the Fourth of July, only a single day of attendance at my office would have been lost. Best of all, it would have cost nothing.

Dora has a great deal of work to do; but she neglects nothing appertaining to my comfort. Aunty 'Ouisa has favored me with one cup of coffee, since thou wentest away, and with an occasional doughnut; but I think thy lectures on diet and regimen have produced a considerable effect.

Dearest, is thy absence so nearly over that we can now see light glimmering at the end of it? Is it half over? If not, I really do not see how I am to bear it. A month of non-existence is the utmost limit——

I am continually interrupted as I write, this being pay-day, and a very busy time. I don't know exactly what will be the amount of our fees; but I should think it would be about as good a month as the last. Thirty-five dollars, however, have already been drawn for our quarter's rent. If thou wantest any more money, as probably thou dost, write me how much, and I will send it. How much must I reserve to pay Rebecca's wages? Any surplus, I intend to apply in lessening Millet's bill.

Here comes somebody else. 190

Ownest wife,

I am the best, and truest, and lovingest husband that ever was, because thy goodness makes me so.

Mrs. Sophia A. Hawthorne,
West Newton, Mass.

TO MRS. HAWTHORNE

Surveyor's Office, July 5th, 1848

Unspeakably belovedest, thy letter has just been handed me, and I snatch a moment from much press of business to say a word to thee. It has made my heart heave like the sea, it is so tender and sweet. Ah, thou hast my whole soul. There is no thinking how much I love thee; and how blessed thy love makes me. I wonder how thou canst love me.

Thy letter was also most comfortable to me, because it gives such a picture of thy life there with the children. It seemed as if I could see the whole family of my heart before my eyes, and could hear you all talking together. I began to be quite uneasy about little Bundlebreech's indisposition, until thy latest intelligence reassured me. Yet I shall be anxious to hear again.

Dora could not come to Boston yesterday, to meet Rebecca, because she has an infinity of 192 work, and moreover, yesterday morning, she had to go to bed with the tooth-ache.

I went to Boston to see the fireworks, and got home between 11 & 12 o'clock, last evening. I went into the little room to put on my linen coat; and, on my return into the sitting room, behold! a stranger there—whom dost thou think it might be?—it was Elizabeth! I did not wish to risk frightening her away by anything like an exhibition of wonder; and so we greeted one another kindly and cordially, but with no more *empressement* than if we were constantly in the habit of meeting. It being so late, and I so tired, we did not have much talk then; but she said she meant to go to walk this afternoon, and asked me to go with her—which I promised to do. Perhaps she will now make it her habit to come down and see us occasionally in the evening.

Oh, my love, my heart calls for thee so, that I know not how to wait weeks longer for thee. Yet I would not that thou shouldst deprive the children of the beautiful country on that account. All will be repaid us in the first hour of meeting.

Own wife, the coat does not crock the shirtsleeve in the least—so thy labor in lining it would have been thrown away. I gave the vest 193 to Louisa soon after thou wentest away, and have seen nothing of it since.

I wish Una, and Julian too, would write a letter to Aunty 'Ouisa. I know it would give her as much pleasure as anything can.

> With infinite love,
> I am THINE OWNEST.

Naughtiest, I do not leave thy letter about. I would just as soon leave my own heart on the "walking side," as Una calls it.

Mrs. Sophia A. Hawthorne,
West Newton.

TO MRS. HAWTHORNE

Salem, July 7th, 1848

Ownest, when thy letters come, I always feel as if I could not have done without them a moment longer. Thou must have received one from me since the date of thine, but I hope it will not weary thee to receive this brief scribblement. If my hand would only answer to my heart, what letters I should write thee! It is wonderful—the growth of our love! Six years ago, it seemed infinite; yet what was the love of that epoch to the present! Thou badest me burn two pages of thy last letter; but I cannot do it, and will not; for never was a wife's deep, warm, chaste love so well expressed, and it is as holy to me as the Bible. Oh, I cannot begin to tell how I love thee.

Dearest, I should not forgive myself if I were to deprive the children of the country. Thou must keep them there as long as thou canst. When thou hast paid thy visit to Sarah Clark, I 195 must come and see thee in Boston, and if possible (and if I shall be welcome) will spend a Sunday there with thee.

There is no news. Miss Derby has finished her picture, and it is now being publicly exhibited. I have not yet seen it, but mean to go.

Mr. Pike is going to dine with me to-day, on green peas.

Oh, for one kiss!

THY   LOVINGEST
HUSBAND.

Did Julian have a tooth?——or what was the matter? Why did all the children have fever-fits? Why was Horace jumped in a wet sheet?

Mrs. Sophia A. Hawthorne.

TO MRS. HAWTHORNE

Salem, July 12th, 1848

Dearest Phoebe, I enclose an advertisement of silks. Aunty 'Ouisa would like to have you get some patterns of those which she has marked with a pencil.

A letter from Mrs. F. Shaw came for thee to-day; and I opened and read it. It contains nothing that requires thy immediate perusal; and as it is rather bulky, I do not send it. She is well, and so is Caroline Sturgis.

I hear great accounts of the canary birds, now exhibiting in Boston; and it seems to me thou mightest please Una very much by taking her to see them.

I need thee very much indeed, and shall heartily thank God when thou comest back to thine own home—and thine ownest husband. What a wretched time thou art having on that infernal mattress——Truly do I pity thee, cooped up in that hot and dusty house, such a day as this. 197 Were it not for Dr. Wesselhoeft, I should think it best for thee to get away immediately.

Did Una remember me, when she waked up?—and has little Bundlebreech wanted me?—and dost thou thyself think of me with moderate kindness? Oh, Phoebe, it is too great a sacrifice—this whole blank month in our wedded life. I want thee always.

THY LOVINGEST
SPOUSE.

Mrs. Sophia A. Hawthorne,
Care of Dr. N. Peabody,
Boston, Massachusetts.

TO MRS. HAWTHORNE

Belovedest, thy letter came yesterday, and caused my heart to heave like an ocean. Thou writest with a pen of celestial fire;—none ever wrote such letters but thou—none is worthy to read them but I—and I only because thou purifiest and exaltest me by thy love. Angels, I doubt not, are well pleased to look over thy shoulder as thou writest. I verily believe that no mortals, save ourselves, have ever known what enjoyment was. How wonderful that to the pure in spirit all earthly bliss is given in a measure which the voluptuary never can have dreamed of.

Soon—soon—thou wilt be at home. What joy! I count the days, and almost the hours, already. There is one good in our separation—that it has enabled us to estimate whereabouts we are, and what vast progress we have made into the ever-extending infinite of love. Wherefore, 199 this will not be a blank space, but a bright one, in our recollection.

Dearest, I told Louisa of thy wish that she should come on Saturday; and it seemed that the proposal found favor in her eyes. If not, she will perhaps commission thee to buy her a gown.

Elizabeth came down to see me last evening, and we confabulated till eleven o'clock.

Dora is dying to see thee and the children. The fortune teller has foretold that she is not to marry poor Mr. Hooper, nor anybody else that has been hitherto in question; but a young man, who, Dora says, lives in Boston. She has thorough faith in the prediction.

I forgot to take those two volumes of Cooper's Miles Wallingford; and when I was last in Boston, I looked for them on the shelf in vain. If they may conveniently be had, when thou comest home, wilt thou please to give thyself the trouble of taking them.

Kiss our beloved children for me.

Thou art coming home!—Thou art coming home!

THINE OWNEST
HUSBAND.

Mrs. Sophia A. Hawthorne,
Care of Dr. N. Peabody,
Boston, Massachusetts.

TO MRS. HAWTHORNE

Ownest Phoebe,

Thy letter did not come till to-day; and I know not that I was ever more disappointed and impatient—for I was sure that it ought to have come yesterday, and went to the Post Office three times after it. Now I have nothing to tell thee, belovedest wife, but write thee just a word, because I must. Thou growest more and more absolutely essential to me, every day we live. I never knew how thou art intertwined with my being, till this absence.

Darlingest, thou hast mentioned Horace's sickness two or three times, and I have speculated somewhat thereupon. Thou hast removed to West-street, likewise, and reservest the reasons till we meet. I wonder whether there be any connection between these two matters. But I do not feel anxious. If I am not of a hopeful nature, at least my imagination is not suggestive of 201 evil. If Una were to have the hooping-cough, I should be glad thou wast within Dr. Wesselhoeft's sphere.

What a shadowy day is this! While this weather lasts, thou canst not come.

THY   BELOVEDEST
HUSBAND.

Do not hasten home on my account—stay as long as thou deemest good. I well know how thy heart is tugging thee hitherward.

Mrs. Sophia A. Hawthorne,
Care of Dr. N. Peabody,
Boston, Massachusetts.

TO MRS. HAWTHORNE

14   Mull   street,   Monday,
[*Salem,*] 16th April, 1849

Ownest wife,

I suppose thou wilt not expect (nor wish for) a letter from me; but it is so desolate and lonesome here that I needs must write. This is a miserable time. Thy and the children's absence; and this dreary bluster of the wind, which at once exasperates and depresses me to the very last degree; and finally, a breakfast (the repetition of yesterday's) of pease and Indian pudding!! It is a strange miscellany of grievances; but it does my business—it makes me curse my day. This matter of the breakfast is the most intolerable, just at this moment; because the taste of it is still in my mouth, and the nausea and disgust overwhelms me like the consciousness of sin. Hell is nothing else but eating pease and baked Indian pudding! If thou lovest me, never let me see either of them again. Keep such things for thy and my worst enemies. Give thy husband bread, 203 or cold potatoes; and he never will complain—but pease and Indian pudding! God forgive me for ever having burthened my conscience with such abominations. They are the Unpardonable Sin and the Intolerable Punishment, in one and the same accursed spoonfull!

I think I hardly ever had such a dismal time as yesterday. I cannot bear the loneliness of the house. I need the sunshine of the children; even their little quarrels and naughtinesses would be a blessing to me. I need thee, above all, and find myself, at every absence, so much the less able to endure it. Come home come home!

Where dost thou think I was on Saturday afternoon? Thou wilt never guess.

In haste; for it is almost Custom House time.

Mrs. Sophia A. Hawthorne,
Care of Dr. N. Peabody,
13 West Street,
Boston, Mass.

TO MRS. HAWTHORNE

Salem, May 9th, 1849

Dearest,

Thy letter was received last night. What a time thou hast!—and I not there to help thee! I almost feel as if I ought to come every day; but then I should do so little good—arriving at 4 o'clock; and the children going to bed at six or seven; and the expense is so considerable. If thou canst hold out till Friday, I shall endeavor to come in the afternoon and stay till Monday. But this must depend on arrangements hereafter to be made; so do not absolutely expect me before Saturday. Oh that Providence would bring all of you home, before then! This is a miserable time for me; more so than for thee, with all thy toil, and watchfulness and weariness. These sunless days are as sunless within as without. Thou hast no conception how melancholy our house can be. It absolutely chills my heart.

If it is necessary for me to come sooner, write 205 by express. Give my love to Una and Julian, and tell them how much I miss them. God bless thee and them.

Mrs. Sophia A. Hawthorne,
Care of Dr. N. Peabody,

13 West-street,
Boston.

TO MRS. HAWTHORNE

Navy Yard, April 26th, 1850

Ownest wife,

Thy letter (dated 22d, but postmarked this very day) has just arrived, and perplexed me exceedingly with its strange aspect. Thy poor dear thumb! I am afraid it puts thee to unspeakable pain and trouble, and I feel as if I ought to be with thee; especially as Una is not well. What is the matter?—anything except her mouth? I almost wish thou hadst told me to come back.

It rained so continually on the day of my departure that I was not able to get over to the Navy Yard, but had to put up at the Rockingham House. Being recognized there, I was immediately lugged into society, whether I would or no; taking tea at one place, and spending the evening at another. I have since dined out, and been invited to a party—but escaped this latter infliction. Bridge's house, however, is the quietest 207 place imaginable, and I only wish thou couldst be here, until our Lenox home is ready. I long to see thee, and am sad for want of thee. And thou too so comfortless in all that turmoil and confusion!

I have been waiting for thee to write; else I should have written before, though with nothing to say to thee—save the unimportant fact that I love thee better than ever before, and that I cannot be at peace away from thee. Why has not Dr. Wesselhoeft cured thy thumb? Thou never must hereafter do any work whatever; thou wast not made strong, and always sufferest tenfold the value of thy activities. Thou didst much amiss, to marry a husband who cannot keep thee like a lady, as Bridge does his wife, and as I should so delight to keep thee, doing only beautiful things, and reposing in luxurious chairs, and with servants to go and to come. Thou hast a hard lot in life; and so have I that witness it, and can do little or nothing to help thee. Again I wish that thou hadst told me to come back; or, at least, whether I should come or no. Four days more will bring us to the first of May, which is next Wednesday; and it was my purpose to return then. Thou wilt get this letter, I suppose, tomorrow morning, and, if desirable, might send 208 to me by express the same day; and I could leave here on Monday morning. On looking at the Pathfinder Guide, I find that a train leaves Portsmouth for Boston at 5 o'clock P.M. Shouldst thou send me a message by the 11 o'clock train, I might return and be with thee tomorrow (Saturday) evening, before 8 o'clock. I should come without being recalled; only that it seems a sin to add another human being to the multitudinous chaos of that house.

I cannot write. Thou hast our home and all our interests about thee, and away from thee there is only emptiness—so what have I to write about?

THINE   OWNEST
HUSBAND.

P.S. If thou sendest for me to-morrow, and I do not come, thou must conclude that the express did not reach me.

Mrs. Sophia A. Hawthorne,
Care of Dr. Nathl. Peabody,
Boston, Massachusetts

TO MRS. HAWTHORNE

Lenox, July 30th, 1851

Dearest Phoebe,

We are getting along perfectly well, and without a single event that could make a figure in a letter. I keep a regular chronicle of all our doings; and you may read it on your return. Julian seems perfectly happy, but sometimes talks in rather a sentimental style about his mother. I do hope thou camest safely to West Newton, and meetest with no great incommodities there. Julian is now out in the garden; this being the first time since thou wentest away, almost, (except when he was in bed) that he has left me for five minutes together. I find him really quite a tolerable little man!

Kiss Una for me, and believe me,

Thy affectionate
husband,
N. H.

Mrs. Sophia A. Hawthorne,
West Newton.

TO MRS. HAWTHORNE

Dearest Phoebe,

I send the tools, which I found in one of the cupboards. Thy two letters arrived together, this morning. I was at the P. O. on Wednesday, and greatly disappointed to find nothing.

Julian and I get along together in great harmony,& as happy as we can be severed from thee. It grieves me that thou findest nobody to help thee there. If this state of things is to continue, thou must abridge thy stay, and return before thou art quite worn out.

I wrote a few lines on Tuesday (I think) which I suppose thou hast received. I more than ever abhor letter-writing; but thou partly knowest that I am

> Thy lovingest
> HUSBAND.

Mrs. Sophia A. Hawthorne,
West Newton.

TO MRS. HAWTHORNE

Lenox, August 7th, 1851.—
Thursday

Ownest Phoebe,

I rec'd thy letter yesterday. I will be in Pittsfield on *Thursday* next (a week from to-day) and will escort thee home.

I have written quite a small volume of Julian's daily life and mine; so that, on thy return, thou wilt know everything that we have done and suffered;—as to enjoyment, I don't remember to have had any, during thy absence. It has been all doing and suffering.

Thou sayest nothing whatever of Una.

Unless I receive further notice from thee I shall consider Thursday the day. I shall go at any rate, I think, rain or shine; but of course, thou wilt not start in a settled rain. In that case, I shall come again to Pittsfield, the next day. But, if fair weather, I hope nothing will detain thee; or if it necessarily must, and thou 212 has[t] previous knowledge of it, thou canst write me.

Julian is perfectly well. We both, according to our respective capacities, long for thee.

TO MRS. HAWTHORNE

Lenox, August 8th, 1851

Ownest Phoebe,

I wrote thee a note yesterday, and sent it to the village by Cornelius; but as he may have neglected to put it in, I write again. If thou wilt start from West Newton on *Thursday* next, I will meet thee at Pittsfield, which will answer the same purpose as if I came all the way.

Mrs. Tappan requests that thou wilt bring ten pounds of ground rice for her; or a less quantity, if thou hast not room for so much.

Julian is very well, and keeps himself happy from morning till night. I hope Una does the same. Give my love to her.

I shall be most gladdest to see thee.

August 9th.—Saturday.—I recd. yesterday 214 thy note, in which thou speakest of deferring thy return some days longer. Stay by all means as long as may be needful. Julian gets along perfectly well; and I am eager for thy coming only because it is unpleasant to remain torn asunder. Thou wilt write to tell me finally what day thou decidest upon;—but unless I hear from thee, I shall go to Pittsfield on *Saturday*, a week from to-day. But if thou seest reason for staying longer do so, that nothing may be left at loose ends.

Julian and I had a fine ride yesterday with Herman Melville and two other gentlemen.

Mrs. Peters is perfectly angelic.

TO MRS. HAWTHORNE

West Newton, Septr. 19th, 1851

Dearest Phoebe,

Here I am as thou seest; and if not here, I know not where I could be; for Boston is so full that the Mayor has issued proclamation for the inhabitants to throw open their doors. The President is there.

They all appear to be well here; and thy mother, if Horace and Georgia say truly, walked three miles yesterday. I went with Mary to see her, last evening, and found her much better than I ever hoped.

Talking with Mary, last night, I explained our troubles to her, and our wish to get away from Lenox, and she renewed the old proposition about our taking this house for the winter. The great objection to it, when first talked of, was, that we, or I, did not wish to have the care and responsibility of your father and mother. That is now removed. It 216 strikes me as one of those unexpected, but easy and natural solutions wherewith Providence occasionally unknots a seemingly inextricable difficulty. If you agree with me, you had better notify Mr. or Mrs. Sedgwick that we shall not want the Kemble house. We can remain in the red house till we come here.

We shall pay a rent, but I know not as yet precisely what. But we shall probably only remain half the time Mr. and Mrs. Mann are in Washington.

Mary will write.

I shall probably go to Salem on Saturday. Kiss and spank the children.

Thine ownest in haste,
N. H.

Mrs. Sophia A. Hawthorne,
Lenox, Massachusetts.

TO MRS. HAWTHORNE

Salem, Sept. 23^d, 1851

Dearest,

I have just received thy two letters; they having been forwarded hither by Ticknor & Co. I wish thou hadst not had the head-ache; it gives me the heart-ache.

In regard to the rent, it is much to pay; but thou art to remember that we take the house only till we can get another; and that we shall not probably have to pay more than half, at most, of the $350. It does seem to me better to go; for we shall never be comfortable in Lenox again. Ticknor & Co. promise the most liberal advances of money, should we need it, towards buying the house.

I will tell thee my adventures when I come. 218 I am to return to Boston to-night, and fully intend to be in Lenox by Saturday night.

In hugest haste,
THINE OWNEST.

Mrs. Sophia A. Hawthorne,
Lenox, Massachusetts.

TO MRS. HAWTHORNE

Portsmouth, Sept. 3^d, 1852

Ownest Phoebe,

I left Brunswick Wednesday night, and arrived here yesterday, with Pierce. My adventures thou shalt know when I return, and how I was celebrated by orators and poets—and how, by the grace of Divine Providence, I was not present, to be put to the blush. All my contemporaries have grown the funniest old men in the world. Am I a funny old man?

I am going to cross over to the Isle of Shoals, this forenoon, and intend to spend several days there, until I get saturated with sea-breezes.

I love thee very much-est;—likewise, the children are very pleasant to think of. Kiss Una—Kiss Julian—Kiss Rosebud—for me! Kiss thyself, if thou canst—and I wish thou wouldst kiss me.

A boat passes between Portsmouth and the Isle 220 of Shoals, every forenoon; and a letter, I presume, would reach me in case of necessity.

I long to see thee. It is breakfast time.

Mrs. Sophia A. Hawthorne,
Concord, Massachusetts.

TO MRS. HAWTHORNE

New York, Sunday morng.,
April 17th, 1853

Dearest,

I arrived here in good condition Thursday night at ½ past 12. Every moment of my time has been so taken up with calls and engagements that I really could not put pen to paper until now, when I am writing before going down to breakfast.

It is almost as difficult to see O'Sullivan here as if he were a hundred miles off. I rode three miles to his home on Friday, and found him not at home. However, he came yesterday, and we talked together until other people came between.

I do wish I could be let alone, to follow my own ideas of what is agreeable. To-day, I am to dine with a college-professor of mathematics, to meet Miss Lynch!! Why did I ever leave thee, my own dearest wife? Now, thou seest, I am to be lynched.

We have an ugly storm here to-day. I intend 222 to leave New York for Philadelphia tomorrow, and shall probably reach Washington on Wednesday.

I am homesick for thee. The children, too, seem very good and beautiful. I hope Una will be very kind and sweet. As for Julian, let Ellen make him a pandowdy. Does Rosebud still remember me? It seems an age since I left home.

No words can tell how I love thee. I will write again as soon as possible.

THINE   OWNEST HUSBAND.

TO MRS. HAWTHORNE

Philadelphia, Tuesday 19th, 1853

Ownest,

We left New York yesterday at 3 o'clock, and arrived safely here, where we have spent the day. We leave for Washington tomorrow morning, and I shall mail this scribble there, so that thou wilt know that I have arrived in good condition. Thou canst not imagine the difficulty of finding time and place to write a word. I enjoy the journey and seeing new places, but need thee beyond all possibility of telling. I feel as if I had just begun to know that there is nothing else for me but thou. The children, too, I know how to love, at last. Kiss them all for me. In greatest haste (and in a public room),

Baltimore, Wednesday, 5 o'clock.—Thus far in safety. I shall mail the letter immediately 224 on reaching Washington, where we expect to be at ½ past 9.

With love a thousand times more than ever,

Washington, Thursday.—Before Breakfast.

—Dearest, I arrived so late and tired, last night, that I quite forgot to mail the letter. I found about a dozen letters awaiting me at the hotel, from other people, but none from thee. My heart is weary with longing for thee. I want thee in my arms.

I shall go to the President at nine o'clock this morning—shall spend three or four days here—and mean to be back early next week.

TO MRS. HAWTHORNE

Washington, April 28th, Thursday. 1853

Dearest,

The President has asked me to remain in the city a few days longer, for particular reasons; but I think I shall be free to leave by Saturday. It is very queer how much I have done for other people and myself since my arrival here. Colonel Miller is to be here to-night. Ticknor stands by me manfully, and will not quit me until we see Boston again.

I went to Mount Vernon yesterday with the ladies of the President's family. Thou never sawst such a beautiful and blossoming Spring as we have here.

Expect me early in next week. How I long to be in thy arms is impossible to tell. Tell the children I love them all.

TO MRS. HAWTHORNE

Liverpool, July 26th, '54

Dearest Wife,

We had the pleasantest passage, yesterday, that can be conceived of. How strange, that the best weather I have ever known should have come to us on these English coasts!

I enclose some letters from the O'Sullivan's, whereby you will see that they have come to a true appreciation of Mr. Cecil's merits. They say nothing of his departure; but I shall live in daily terror of his arrival.

I hardly think it worth while for me to return to the island, this summer;—that is, unless you conclude to stay longer than a week from this time. Do so, by all means, if you think the residence will benefit either yourself or the children. Or it would be easy to return thither, should it seem desirable—or to go somewhere else. Tell me what day you fix upon for leaving; and I will either await you in person at the landing-place, 227 or send Henry. Do not start, unless the weather promises to be favorable, even though you should be all ready to go on board.

I think you should give something to the servants—those of them, at least, who have taken any particular pains with you. Michael asked me for something, but I told him that I should probably be back again;—so you must pay him my debts and your own too.

It is very lonesome at Rock Ferry, and I long to have you all back again. Give my love to the children..

TO MRS. HAWTHORNE

Liverpool, Sept. 12th, 1854

Dearest,

We arrived safe at Rock Ferry at about ten. Emily had gone to bed, but came down in her night-clothes—the queerest figure I ever saw.

I enclose a letter from thy brother N. It contains one piece of intelligence very interesting to the parties concerned.

Mr. O'Sullivan is going to London, this afternoon. I wish thou wast at home, for the house is very cheerless in its solitude. But it will be only a few days before I see thee again; and in the meantime thou must go to all accessible places, and enjoy thyself for both of us. The barometer goes backward to-day, and indicates a proximate change of weather. What wilt thou do in a rain-storm?

I am weighed down and disheartened by the 229 usual immense pile of American newspapers. What a miserable country!

Kiss all the old people for me—Julian, as well as the others.

TO MRS. HAWTHORNE

Dearest,

I slept at Lancaster, last night, where I arrived at 10 o'clock; and leaving at ½ past nine, this morning, got here at twelve.

Since leaving you, I have been thinking that we have skimmed the cream of the lakes, and perhaps may as well go somewhere else, now. What if you should come to Liverpool (that is, to Rock Ferry Hotel) and spend a day or two, for the sake of variety, and then go to Matlock or Malvern, or wherever we may think best? Should you conclude to do this, I think you had better take a phaeton & pair from Grasmere to Windermere, and there you can get on the rail. If you wish to stay longer at the lakes, however, I shall be quite happy to come back. Mr. Wildeys says that lodgings may be had reasonable (and some at farmers' houses) in the vicinity of 231 Bourness; but he does not know of any in particular.

Weigh these matters, and decide for yourself. I have an impression, I hardly know why, that we have done with the lakes for this year; but I should not regret to have you stay longer.

I send the halves of a £10 & of a £5.

There would be no difficulty in your coming here without a male attendant.

Do not think that I wish you to come, contrary to your opinion. If you and the children are comfortable & happy, I am quite content to take another draught of the lakes.

Kiss them all.

Mr. Bradford and Miss Ripley sailed a fortnight ago.

Mr. Bright was in this morning.

TO MRS. HAWTHORNE

Liverpool, Novr. 3^d, 1855

Dearest wife,

I received your letter a week ago, telling me of your woeful passage and safe arrival. If I had thought how much you were to suffer on the voyage, I never could have consented to thy departure; but I hope thou art now flourishing in the southern sunshine, and I am sure it would have been a dreadful matter for thee to remain in such weather as we have lately had. But I do so long to see thee! If it were not for Julian, I do not think I could bear it at all. He is really a great comfort and joy to me, and rather unexpectedly so; for I must confess I wished to keep him here on his own account and thine, much more than on my own. We live together in great love and harmony, the best friends in the world. He has begun to go to dancing-school; and I have heard of a drawing-master for him, but do not yet let him take lessons, because they 233 might interfere with his day-school, should we conclude to send him thither. His health and spirits seem now to be perfectly good; and I think he is benefitted by a greater regularity of eating than when at home. He never has anything between meals, and seems not to want anything. Mrs. Blodgett, Miss Williams, and their niece, all take motherly care of him, combing his wool, and seeing that he looks clean and gentlemanly as a Consul's son ought to do. Since the war-cloud has begun to darken over us, he insists on buckling on his sword the moment he is dressed, and never lays it aside till he is ready to go to bed—after drawing it, and making blows and thrusts at Miss Williams's tom-cat, for lack of a better antagonist. I trust England and America will have fought out their warfare before his worship's beard begins to sprout; else he will pester us by going forth to battle.

I crossed over to Rock Ferry, a few days ago; and thou canst not imagine the disgust and horror with which I greeted that abominable old pier. The atmosphere of the river absolutely sawed me asunder. If we had been wise enough to avoid the river, I believe thou wouldst have found the climate of England quite another thing; for though we have had very bad weather for weeks 234 past, the air of the town has nothing like the malevolence of that of the river. Mrs. Hantress is quite well, and inquires very affectionately about thee, and the children, and Fanny. Mrs. Watson crossed in the same boat with me. She has taken a house at Cloughton, and was now going over to deliver up the keys of the Rock Ferry house. I forgot to inquire about Miss Sheppard, and do not know whether she has succeeded in letting our house.

I dined at Mr. Bright's on Thursday evening. Of course, there were the usual expressions of interest in thy welfare; and Annie desired to be remembered to Una. Mr. Channing called on me, a few days since. He has just brought his family from Southport, where they have been spending several weeks. Our conversation was chiefly on the subject of the approaching war; for there has suddenly come up a mysterious rumor and ominous disturbance of all men's spirits, as black and awful as a thunder-gust. So far as I can ascertain, Mr. Buchanan considers the aspect of affairs very serious indeed; and a letter, said to be written with his privity, was communicated to the Americans here, telling of the breach of treaties, and a determination on the part of the British Government to force us 235 into war. It will need no great force, however, if the Yankees are half so patriotic at home, as we on this side of the water. We hold the fate of England in our hands, and it is time we crushed her—blind, ridiculous, old lump of beef, sodden in strong beer, that she is; not but what she has still vitality enough to do us a good deal of mischief, before we quite annihilate her.

At Mr. Bright's table, for the first time, I heard the expression of a fear that the French alliance was going to be ruinous to England, and that Louis Napoleon was getting his arm too closely about the neck of Britannia, insomuch that the old lady will soon find herself short of breath. I think so indeed! He is at the bottom of these present commotions.

One good effect of a war would be, that I should speedily be warned out of England, and should betake myself to Lisbon. But how are we to get home? Luckily, I don't care much about getting home at all; and we will be cosmopolites, and pitch our tent in any peaceable and pleasant spot we can find, and perhaps get back to Concord by the time our larch-trees have ten years' growth. Dost thou like this prospect?

What a beautiful letter was thine! I do think nobody else ever wrote such letters, so magically 236 descriptive and narrative. I have read it over and over and over to myself, and aloud to Julian, whose face shone as he listened. By-the-by, I meant that he should have written a letter to accompany this; but this is his dancing-school day, and I did not bring him to the Consulate. One packet of letters, intended for Lisbon, has mysteriously vanished; and I cannot imagine what has become of it, unless it were slipt by mistake into Ticknor's letter-bag, and so went to America by the last steamer. It contained a letter from thy sister Elizabeth, one from Julian, and myself, and, I believe, one from Mr. Dixon.

Did you pay a bill (of between one or two pounds) of Frisbie, Dyke & Co.? I inquired in my last about Mr. Weston's bill for coals.

Do not stint thyself on the score of expenses, but live and dress and spend like a lady of station. It is entirely reasonable and necessary that thou shouldst. Send Una to whatever schools, and let her take whatever lessons, thou deemest good.

Kiss Una; kiss naughty little Rosebud. Give my individual love to everybody.

THINE OWN, OWNEST,
OWNESTEST. 237

P.S. Since writing the above, Mr. Channing has been in, and thou wouldst be (as I am) at once confounded and delighted to hear the warlike tone in which he talks. He thinks that the Government of England is trying to force us into a war, and he says, in so many words, "LET IT COME!!!" He is already considering how he is to get home, and says that he feels ready to enlist; and he breathes blood and vengeance against whomsoever shall molest our shores. Huzza! Huzza! I begin to feel warlike, too. There was a rumor yesterday, that our minister had demanded his passports; and I am mistaken in Frank Pierce if Mr. Crampton has not already been ejected from Washington.

No doubt O'Sullivan's despatches will enable him to give thee more authentic intelligence than I possess as to the real prospects.

TO MRS. HAWTHORNE

Liverpool, February 7th, 1856

Thy letter, my own most beloved, (dated Jany. 31st) arrived yesterday, and revived me at once out of a state of half-torpor, half misery—just as much of each as could co-exist with the other. Do not think that I am always in that state; but one thing, dearest, I have been most thoroughly taught by this separation—that is, the absolute necessity of expression. I must tell thee I love thee. I must be told that thou lovest me. It must be said in words and symbolized with caresses; or else, at last, imprisoned Love will go frantic, and tear all to pieces the heart that holds it. And the only other alternative is to be torpid. I just manage to hold out from one letter of thine to another; and then comes life and joy again. Thou canst not conceive what an effect yesterday's letter had on me. It renewed my youth, and made my step lighter; it absolutely gave me an appetite; and I went to 239 bed joyfully to think of it. Oh, my wife, why did God give thee to poor unworthy me! Art thou sure that He made thee for me? Ah, thy intuition must have been well-founded on this point; because, otherwise, all through eternity, thou wouldst carry my stain upon thee; and how could thine own angel ever need thee then! Thou art mine!—Thou *shalt* be mine! Thou hast given thyself to me irredeemably. Thou hast grown to me. Thou canst never get away.

Oh, my love, it is a desperate thing that I cannot see thee this very instant. Dost thou ever feel, at one and the same moment, the impossibility of doing without me, and also the impossibility of having me? I know not how it is that my strong wishes do not bring thee here bodily, while I am writing these words. One of the two impossibilities must needs be overcome; and it seems the strongest impossibility that thou shouldst be anywhere else, when I need thee so insufferably.

Well, my own wife, I have a little wreaked myself now, and will go on more quietly with what I have further to say. As regards O'Sullivan—(how funny that thou shouldst put quotation marks to this name, as if astonished at my calling him so! Did we not entirely agree in 240 thinking "John" an undue and undesirable familiarity? But thou mayst call him "John," or "Jack" either, as best suits thee.)—as regards O'Sullivan, then, my present opinion of him is precisely what thou thyself didst leave upon my mind, in our discussions of his character. I have often had a similar experience before, resulting from thy criticism upon any views of mine. Thou insensibly convertest me to thy own opinion, and art afterwards surprised to find it so; in fact, I seldom am aware of the change in my own mind, until the subject chances to come up for further discussion, and I find myself on what was thy side.

But I will try to give my true idea of his character. I know that he has most vivid affections—a quick, womanly sensibility—a light and tender grace, which, in happy circumstances, would make all his deeds and demonstrations beautiful. In respect to companionship, beyond all doubt, he has never been in such fortunate circumstances as during his present intercourse with thee; and I am willing to allow that thou bringest out his angelic part, and therefore canst not be expected to see anything but an angel in him. It has sometimes seemed to me that the lustre of his angel-plumage has been a little dimmed—his 241 heavenly garments a little soiled and bedraggled—by the foul ways through which it has been his fate to tread, and the foul companions with whom necessity and politics have brought him acquainted. But I had rather thou shouldst take *him* for a friend than any other man I ever knew (unless, perhaps, George Bradford, who can hardly be reckoned a man at all,) because I think the Devil has a smaller share in O'Sullivan than in other bipeds who wear breeches. To do him justice, he is miraculously pure and true, considering what his outward life has been. Now, dearest, I have a genuine affection for him, and a confidence in his honor; and as respects his defects in everything that concerns pecuniary matters, I believe him to have kept his integrity intact to a degree that is really wonderful, in spite of the embarrassments of a lifetime. If we had his whole life mapped out before us, I should probably forgive him some things which thy severer sense of right would condemn. Thou talkest of his high principle; but that does not appear to me to be his kind of moral endowment. Perhaps he may have the material that principles are manufactured from.

My beloved, he is not the man in whom I see my ideal of a friend; not for his lack of principle, 242 not for any ill-deeds or practical shortcomings which I know of or suspect; not but what he is amiable, loveable, fully capable of self-sacrifice, utterly incapable of selfishness. The only reason, that I can put into words, is, that he never stirs me to any depth beneath my surface; I like him, and enjoy his society, and he calls up, I think, whatever small part of me is elegant and agreeable; but neither of my best nor of my worst has he ever, or could he ever, have a glimpse. I should wish my friend of friends to be a sterner and grimmer man than he; and it is my opinion, sweetest wife, that the truest manly delicacy is to be found in those stern, grim natures—a little alpine flower, of tenderest texture, and loveliest hue, and delicious fragrance, springing out of a rocky soil in a high, breezy, mountain atmosphere. O'Sullivan's quick, genial soil produces an abundant growth of flowers, but not just this precious little flower. He is too much like a woman, without being a woman; and between the two characters, he misses the quintessential delicacy of both. There are some tests of thorough refinement which, perhaps, he could not stand. And yet I shall not dispute that for refinement and delicacy he is one out of a thousand; and we might spend a lifetime together 243 without putting him to a test too severe. As for his sympathies, he would be always ready to pour them out (not exactly like Niagara, but like a copious garden-fountain) for those he loved.

If thou thinkest I have done him great injustice in the foregoing sketch, it is very probable that thou wilt bring me over to thy way of thinking; and perhaps balance matters by passing over to mine.

Dearest, I do hope I shall next hear of thee from Madeira; for this suspense is hard to bear. Thou must not mind what I say to thee, in my impatient agonies, about coming back. Whatever can be borne, I shall find myself able to bear, for the sake of restoring thee to health. I have now groped so far through the thick darkness that [a] little glimmer of light begins to appear at the other end of the passage; it will grow clearer and brighter continually, and at last it will show me my dearest wife. I do hope thou wilt find thy husband wiser and better than he has been hitherto; wiser, in knowing the more adequately what a treasure he has in thee; and better, because I feel it such a shame to be loved by thee without deserving it. Dost thou love me?

Give my love to Una, to whom I cannot write 244 now, without doubling the postage. Do not let little Rosebud forget me. Remember me to Fanny, and present my regards to Madame O'Sullivan, and Mrs. Susan, and Miss Rodgers. So all is said very properly.

Thou toldest me not to write to Madeira before hearing from thee there; but I shall send this to the care of the American Consul, to whom I wrote by the last Lisbon steamer, sending the letter to O'Sullivan's care. Thine own-ownest.

Julian is perfectly well. 245

TO MRS. HAWTHORNE

Liverpool, March 18th, 1856

In a little while longer, ownest wife, we must think about thy return to England. The thought is a happiness greater than I can crowd into my mind. Wilt thou think it best to go back to Lisbon? This must depend, I suppose, on the length of stay of the O'Sullivans in Madeira. If they return to Lisbon before June, thou wilt have to go with them; if they stay so late as the first of June, I should think it best for thee to come direct to Southampton; but I leave it to thy decision, as thou canst weigh all the circumstances. I somewhat dread thy returning to this miserable island at all; for I fear, even if Madeira quite rids thee of thy cough, England will at once give it back. But Elizabeth has sent thee a certain article which is vouched for, by numerous certificates, as a certain cure for all coughs and affections of the lungs. So far as I can ascertain its structure, it consists of some layers 246 of quilted flannel, covered with an oilcloth; and the whole thing is not more than three inches square. It is worn on the breast, next the skin, and, being so small, it would not be perceptible under the thinnest dress. In order to make it efficacious, it is to be moistened with some liquor from a bottle which accompanied it; and it keeps the person comfortably warm, and appears to operate like a charm, and makes a little Madeira of its own about the wearer. If thou wast not so very naughty—if thou wouldst consent to be benefitted by anything but homeopathy—here in this little box is health and joy for us!—yes, the possibility of sitting down together in a mud-puddle, or in the foggiest hole in England, and being perfectly well and happy. Oh, mine ownest love, I shall clap this little flannel talisman upon thy dearest bosom, the moment thou dost touch English soil. Every instant it shall be shielded by the flannel. I have drawn the size and thickness of it, above.

We are plodding on here, Julian and I, in the same dull way. The old boy, however, is happy enough; and I must not forget to tell thee that Mary W. has taken him into her good graces, and has quite thrown off another boy, who, Julian says, has heretofore been her "adorer." I 247 told Julian that he must expect to be cast aside in favor of somebody else, by-and-bye. "Then I shall tell her that I am very much ashamed of her," said he. "No," I answered; "you must bear it with a good grace and not let her know that you are mortified." "But why shouldn't I let her know it, if I *am* mortified?" asked he; and really, on consideration, I thought there was more dignity and self-respect in his view of the case, than in mine; so I told him to act as he thought right. But I don't think he will be much hurt or mortified; for his feelings are marvellously little interested, after all, and he sees her character and criticises her with a shrewdness that quite astonishes me. He is a wonderfully observant boy; nothing escapes his notice; nothing, hardly, deceives his judgment. His intellect is certainly very remarkable, and it is almost a miracle to see it combined with so warm and true and simple a heart. But his heart admits very few persons into it, large though it be. He is not, I think, of a diffusive, but of a concentrative tendency, both as regards mind and affections.

In Grace Greenwood's last "Little Pilgrim," there is a description of her new baby!!! in response to numerous inquiries which, she says, have been received from her subscribers. I wonder 248 she did not think it necessary to be brought to bed in public, or, at least, in presence of a committee of the subscribers. My dearest, I cannot enough thank God, that, with a higher and deeper intellect than any other woman, thou hast never—forgive me the base idea!—never prostituted thyself to the public, as that woman has, and as a thousand others do. It does seem to me to deprive women of all delicacy. Women are too good for authorship, and that is the reason it spoils them so.

The Queen of England is said to be going to Lisbon, this summer; so perhaps thou wouldst rather stay there and be introduced to her, than come hither and be embraced by me—The O'Sullivans would not miss seeing her, I suppose, for all the husbands on earth. Dearest, I do not like those three women very much; and, indeed, they cannot be good and amiable, nor wise, since, after living with thee for months, they have not made thee feel that they value thee above all things else. Neither am I satisfied with Mr. Welsh's turning thee out of his house.

Mr. Dallas, our new Ambassador, arrived at Liverpool a few days ago; and I had to be civil to him and his son, and to at least five ladies whom he brought with him. He seems to be a 249 good old gentleman enough, and of venerable aspect; but as regards ability, I should judge Mr. Buchanan to be worth twenty of him. Dost thou know that we are going to have a war? It is now quite certain; and I hope I shall be ordered out of the country in season to meet thee at Madeira. Dost thou not believe me?

March 19th.—Ownest beloved, this morning came thy letter of the 9th, by the African steamer. I knew it could not be much longer delayed, for my heart was getting intolerably hungry. Oh, my wife, thou hast been so ill! And thou art blown about the world, in the midst of rain and whirlwind! It was a most foolish project of O'Sullivan's (as all his projects are) to lead thee from his comfortable fireside, to that comfortless Madeira. And thou sayest, or Una says, that the rainy season is just commencing there, and that this month and the next are the two worst months of the year! Thou *never* again shalt go away anywhere without me. My two arms shall be thy tropics, and my breast thy equator; and from henceforth forever I will keep thee a great deal too warm, so that thou shalt cry out—"Do let me breathe the cool outward air for a moment!" But I will not.

As regards teaching Julian French, I wish I 250 had found a master for him when we first left thee; but there seemed to be so many difficulties in making him really and seriously study, without companions, and without constant supervision, that I let it alone, thinking that, on the continent, all lost time would quickly be made up. And now it will be so little while before thy return, that I doubt whether much would be accomplished in the meantime. It is very difficult to get him really interested in any solitary study; and as he could not take more than two lessons in a week, and would have nobody to practise pronounciation with, in the intervals, I think, the result would be only an ineffectual commencement. I have not myself the slightest tact or ability in making him study, or in compelling him to do anything that he is not inclined to do of his own accord; and to tell thee the truth, he has pretty much his own way in everything. At least, such is my impression; but thou hast so often told me of the strength of my will (of which I am not in the least conscious) that it is very possible I may have been ruling him with a rod of iron, all the time. It is true, I have a sort of inert and negative power, with which I should strongly interpose to keep him out of mischief; but I am always inclined to let him wander 251 around at his own sweet will, as long as the path is a safe one. Thou hast incomparably greater faculty of command than I have.

I think he must remain untaught till thou comest back to take the helm. Thou wilt find him a good and honest boy, healthy in mind, and healthier in heart than when he left thee; ready to begin his effectual education as soon as circumstances will permit. Let this suffice. In body, too, he never was better in his life than now; and he is a real little rampant devil for physical strength. I find it an arduous business, now-a-days, to take him across my knee and spank him; and unless I give up the attempt betimes, he will soon be the spanker, and his poor father the spankee.

I am going to dine at Mr. Bright's, this evening. He has often besought me that Julian might come and spend a few days at Sandheys; and I think I shall let him go, and take the opportunity to run up to London. What vicissitudes of country and climate thou hast run through, while I have never once stirred out of this mud and fog of Liverpool! After returning from London, and as Spring advances, I mean to make little excursions of a day or two with Julian. 252

Oh, dearest, dearest, interminably and infinitely dearest—I don't know how to end that ejaculation. The use of kisses and caresses is, that they supersede language, and express what there are no words for. I need them at this moment—need to give them, & to receive them.

TO MRS. HAWTHORNE

32, St. Anne's Place, *London*,
April 7th, 1856

Best wife in the world, here I am in London; for I found it quite impossible to draw any more breath in that abominable Liverpool without allowing myself a momentary escape into better air. I could not take Julian with me; and so I disposed of him, much to his own satisfaction, first with the Brights, then with the Channings; and I have now been here more than a week, and shall remain till Thursday. The old boy writes to me in the best of spirits; and I rather think he can do without me better than I can without him; for I really find I love him *a little*, and that his society is one of my necessities, including, as he does, thyself and everything else that I love. Nevertheless, my time has been so much occupied in London, that I have not been able to brood over the miseries of heart-solitudes. They have found me out, these London people, and I believe I should have engagements for every day, 254 and two or three a day, if I staid here through the season. They thicken upon me, the longer I remain. To-night, I am to dine with the Lord Mayor, and shall have to make a speech!! Good Heavens! I wish I might have been spared this. Tomorrow night, I shall dine in the House of Commons, with a member of Parliament, in order to hear a debate. In short, I have been lionized, and am still being lionized; and this one experience will be quite sufficient for me. I find it something between a botheration and a satisfaction.

Oh, my dearest, I feel that my heart will be very heavy, as soon as I get back to Liverpool; for thy cough is not getting better, and our dear little Rosebud has been ill! And I was not there! And I do not know—and shall not know for many days—what may have since happened to her and thee! This is very hard to bear. We ought never, never, to have separated. It is most unnatural. It cannot be borne. How strange that it *must* be borne!

Most beloved, I have sent down to Liverpool for Elizabeth's talisman and medicine-bottles; for Mr. Marsh is now in London, and perhaps he will be able to take them to thee. I fear, however, that they will not reach me in time to be delivered to 255 him, and I shall be afraid to trust them to any but a private conveyance. If they come, I hope thou wilt give them a fair trial, at least, if the weather still continues cold and wet. What a wretched world we live in! Not one little nook or corner where thou canst draw a wholesome breath! In all our separation, I have never once felt so utterly desperate as at this moment. I *cannot* bear it.

Everybody inquires about thee. I spent yesterday (Sunday) at Mrs. S. C. Hall's country-seat, and she was very affectionate in her inquiries, and gave me this very sheet of paper on which I am now writing—also some violets, which I have lost, though I promised faithfully to send them to Madeira. Dear me, I wish I had a little bit of sentiment! Didst thou ever read any of her books? She is a very good and kind person, and so is her husband, though he besmeared me with such sweetness of laudation, that I feel all over bestuck, as after handling sweetmeats or molasses-candy. There is a limit of decorum which ought not to be over-stept.

I met Miss Cushman, on Saturday, in the Strand, and she asked me to dinner, but I could not go, being already engaged to meet another actress! I have a strange run of luck as regards actresses, having made friends with the three most 256 prominent ones since I came to London, and I find them all excellent people; and they all inquire for thee!! Mrs. Bennoch, too, wishes to see thee very much. Unless thou comest back in very vigorous health, it will never do for us to take lodgings in London for any considerable time, because it would be impossible to keep quiet. Neither shall I dare to have thee come back to Liverpool, accursed place that it is! We will settle ourselves in the South of England, until the autumn, and then (unless Elizabeth's talisman works miracles) we must be gone. The trip to Scotland, I fear, must be quite given up. I suppose, as regards climate, Scotland is only a more intensely disagreeable England.

Oh, my wife, I do want thee so intolerably. Nothing else is real, except the bond between thee and me. The people around me are but shadows. I am myself but a shadow, till thou takest me in thy arms, and convertest me into substance. Till thou comest back, I do but walk in a dream.

I think a great deal about poor little Rosebud, and find that I loved her about ten million times as much as I had any idea of. Really, dearest wife, I have a heart, although, heretofore, thou hast had great reason to doubt it. But it yearns, and throbs, and burns with a hot fire, for thee, and 257 for the children that have grown out of our loves. Una, too! I long unutterably to see her, and cannot bear to think that she has been growing out of her childhood, all the time, without my witnessing each day's change. But the first moment, when we meet again, will set everything right. Oh, blessed moment!

Well, dearest, I must close now, and go in search of Mr. Marsh, whom I have not yet been able to see. God bless thee! I cannot see why He has permitted so much rain, and such cold winds, where thou art.

THINE OWNEST,
OWNEST.

I have no time to read over the above, and know not what I have said, nor left unsaid.

TO MRS. HAWTHORNE

Liverpool, Novr. 24th, 1858

Dearest Wife,

Your letter by the steamer of the 19th has come, and has given me delight far beyond what I can tell thee. There never were such letters in the world as thine; but this, no doubt, I have already told thee over and over. What pleasantly surprises me is, that the beauty of thy hand-writing has all come back, in these Lisbon letters, and they seem precisely the same, in that respect, that my little virgin Dove used to write me.

Before this reaches thee, thou wilt have received the trunks by the Cintra, and also, the sad news of the death of O'Sullivan's brother. I shall wait with the utmost anxiety for thy next letter. Do not thou sympathise too much. Thou art wholly mine, and must not overburthen thyself with anybody's grief—not even that of thy dearest friend next to me. I wish I could be with thee. 259

I am impatient for thee to be well. Thou shouldst not trust wholly to the climate, but must take medical advice—in Lisbon, if it is to be had—otherwise, Dr. Wilkinson's. *Do* take cod-liver oil. It is the only thing I ever really had any faith in; and thou wilt not take it. Thou dost confess to growing thin. Take cod-liver oil, and, at all events, grow fat.

I suppose this calamity of the O'Sullivans will quite shut them up from the world, at present.

Julian thrives, as usual. He has lately been out to dine with a boy of about his own age, in the neighborhood. His greatest daily grievance is, that he is not allowed to have his dinner at 5½, with the rest of the family, but dines at one, and sups alone at our dinner time. He never has anything between meals, unless it be apples. I believe I told thee, in my last, that I had give up the thought of sending him to school, for the present. It would be so great and hazardous a change, in the whole system of his life, that I do not like to risk it as long as he continues to do well. The intercourse which he holds with the people of Mrs. Blodgett's seems to me of a healthy kind. They make a playmate of him, to a certain extent, but do him no mischief; whereas, the best set of boys in the world would infallibly bring him harm as 260 well as good. His manners improve, and I do not at all despair of seeing him grow up a gentleman. It is singular how completely all his affections of the head have disappeared;—and that, too, without any prescriptions from Dr. Dryasdust. I encourage him to make complaints of his health, rather than the contrary; but he always declares himself quite well. The difficulty heretofore has been, I think, that he had grown morbid for want of a wider sphere.

Miss Williams is very unwell, and, for the last two or three days, has had several visits from the Doctor;—being confined to her bed, and in great pain. I don't know what her disorder is; but she is excessively nervous, and is made ill by anything that agitates her. The rumor of war with America confined her for several days.

Give my most affectionate regards to the O'Sullivans. I never felt half so grateful to anybody, as I do to them, for the care they take of thee. It would make a summer climate of Nova Zembla, to say nothing of Lisbon.

P.S. I enclose the gold dollar.

TO MRS. HAWTHORNE

Liverpool, Decr. 11th, 1858

Dearest,

This despatch for O'Sullivan has just reached me; and I do not know whether there will be time to send it by the steamer that sails to-day.

Your letters, written immediately after the receipt of the sad news, did not reach me till yesterday; while those by the Southampton steamer, written afterwards, arrived here days ago. Those Liverpool steamers are not nearly such safe mediums as those by Southampton; and no letters of importance ought to be trusted to them.

Mrs. Blodgett will buy the articles required by Mrs. O'Sullivan, and likewise the soap for you, and have them in readiness for the next Liverpool steamer.

We are quite well (Julian and I) and as contented as we can expect to be, among strangers, and in a continual cold fog. I have heard no private news from America, since I wrote last. 262

I have not a moment's time to write Una; but kiss her for me, and Rosebud too. Neither can I tell thee, in this little moment, how infinitely I love thee.

P.S. Tell O'Sullivan that Mr. Miller (Despatch Agent) will allow the postage of this package in his account with Government.

TO MRS. HAWTHORNE

Liverpool, Decr. 13th, 1858

Dearest,

I wrote thee a brief note by a steamer from this port on the 11th, with O'Sullivan's despatches. Nothing noteworthy has happened since; and nothing can happen in this dawdling[A] life of ours. The best thing about our Liverpool days is, that they are very short; it is hardly morning, before night comes again. Una says that the weather in Lisbon is very cold. So it is here—that searching, spiteful cold that creeps all through one's miserable flesh; and if I had to cross the river, as last winter, I do believe I should drown myself in despair. Nevertheless, Julian and I are in excellent condition, though the old boy often grumbles—"It is very cold, papa!"—as he takes his morning bath.

The other day, speaking of his first advent into this world, Julian said, "I don't remember how I 264 came down from Heaven; but I'm very glad I happened to tumble into so good a family!" He was serious in this; and it is certainly very queer, that, at nearly ten years old, he should still accept literally our first explanation of how he came to be among us.

Thy friend John O'Hara still vagabondises about the street; at least, I met him, some time since, with a basket of apples on his arm, very comfortably clad and looking taller than of yore. I gave him an eleemosynary sixpence, as he told me he was getting on pretty well. Yesterday, his abominable mother laid siege to my office during the greater part of the day, pretending to have business with me. I refused to see her; and she then told Mr. Wilding that her husband was gone to Ireland, and that John was staying at Rock Ferry with Mrs. Woodward, or whatever the lady's name may be, and that she herself had no means of support. But I remained as obdurate as a paving-stone, knowing that, if I yielded this once, she would expect me to supply her with the means of keeping drunk as long as I stay in Liverpool. She hung about the office till dusk, but finally raised the siege.

Julian looks like a real boy now; for Mrs. Blodgett has his hair cut at intervals of a month or so, 265 and though I thought his aspect very absurd, at first, yet I have come to approve it rather than otherwise. The good lady does what she can to keep his hands clean, and his nails in proper condition—for which he is not as grateful as he should be. There is to be a ball at his dancing-school, next week, at which the boys are to wear jackets and white pantaloons; and I have commissioned Miss Maria to get our old gentleman equipped in a proper manner. It is funny how he gives his mighty mind to this business of dancing, and even dreams, as he assured me, about quadrilles. His master has praised him a good deal, and advanced him to a place among his elder scholars. When the time comes for Julian to study in good earnest, I perceive that this feeling of emulation will raise his steam to a prodigious height. In drawing (having no competitors) he does not apply himself so earnestly as to the Terpsichorean science; yet he succeeds so well that, last night, I mistook a sketch of his for one of his master's. Mrs. Blodgett and the ladies think his progress quite wonderful; the master says, rather coolly, that he has a very tolerable eye for form.

Una seems to be taking rapid strides towards womanhood. I shall not see her a child again; 266 that stage has passed like a dream—a dream merging into another dream. If Providence had not done it, as thou sayest, I should deeply regret her having been present at this recent grief-time of the O'Sullivans. It did not seem to me that she needed experiences of that kind; for life has never been light and joyous to her. Her letters make me smile, and sigh, too; they are such letters as a girl of fifteen would write, with a vein of sentiment continually cropping up, as the geologists say, through the surface. Then the religious tone startles me a little. Would it be well—(perhaps it would, I really don't know)—for religion to be intimately connected, in her mind, with forms and ceremonials, and sanctified places of worship? Shall the whole sky be the dome of her cathedral?—or must she compress the Deity into a narrow space, for the purpose of getting at him more readily? Wouldst thou like to have her follow Aunt Lou and Miss Rodgers into that musty old Church of England? This looks very probable to me; but thou wilt know best how it is, and likewise whether it had better be so, or not. If it is natural for Una to remain within those tenets, she will be happiest there; but if her moral and intellectual development should compel her hereafter 267 to break from them, it would be with the more painful wrench for having once accepted them.

December 14th.—Friday.—O'Sullivan desires me to send American newspapers. I shall send some with the parcel by the Liverpool steamer of the 21st; and likewise through John Miller, whenever I have any late ones; but the English Post Office does not recognize American newspapers as being newspapers at all, and will not forward them except for letter postage. This would be ruinous, considering that the rate for single letters, between here and Lisbon, is a shilling and sixpence; and a bundle of newspapers, at a similar rate, would cost several pounds. I *won't* do it.

Miss Williams has not yet left her chamber. Her illness was very serious, and Mrs. Blodgett was greatly alarmed about her; but I believe she is now hopefully convalescent.

Julian is outgrowing all the clothes he has, and is tightening terribly in best sack, and absolutely bursting through his trousers. No doubt thou wouldst blaspheme at his appearance; but all boys are the awkwardest and unbeautifullest creatures whom God has made. I don't know that he looks any worse than the rest. I have given Mrs. Blodgett the fullest liberty to get him whatever 268 she thinks best. He ought to look like a gentleman's son, for the ladies of our family like to have him with them as their cavalier and protector, when they go a-shopping. It amazes me to see the unabashed front with which he goes into society.

I have done my best, in the foregoing scribble, to put thee in possession of the outward circumstances of our position. It is a very dull life; but I live it hopefully, because thou (my true life) will be restored to me by-and-by. If I had known what thou wouldst have to suffer, through thy sympathies, I would not for the world have sent thee to Lisbon; but we were in a strait, and I knew no other way. Take care of thyself for my sake. Remember me affectionately to the O'Sullivans.

On reading over my letter, I cannot make out this word.

TO MRS. HAWTHORNE

31, Hertford St., *London*, May 17th, Thursday [1859]

Dearest,

Una must be tired of the monotony of receiving letters from me; and perhaps thou wilt be willing to relieve her, just for once. Her letter, and Julian's, and Rosebud's, all three gave me great pleasure; and I was particularly astonished at the old boy's learned epistle—so learned, indeed, that it cost me some study to comprehend it. He is certainly a promising lad, and I wish I could answer his letter in Hebrew.

Affairs succeed each other so fast, that I have really forgotten what I did yesterday. I remember seeing Henry Bright, and listening to a stream of babble from his lips, as we strolled in the Park and along the Strand. Today, I have breakfasted with Fields, and met, among other people, Mr. Field Talfourd, who promises to send thee a photograph of his portrait of Mr. Browning. He 270 was very agreeable, and seemed delighted to see me again. At lunch, we had Lady Dufferin, Mrs. Norton, and Mrs. Sterling, author of the Cloister Life of Charles V., with whom we are to dine on Sunday. Thou wouldst be stricken dumb to see how quietly I accept a whole string of invitations, and, what is more, perform my engagements without a murmur.

A little German artist has come to me with a letter of introduction, and a request that I will sit to him for a portrait in bas-relief. To this, likewise, I have consented!!!—Subject to the condition that I shall have my leisure.

Mr. Fields has given me, for thee, The Idylls of the King—not the American, but the English edition.

I have had time to see Bennoch only once. If I go to Canterbury at all, it must be after my visit to Cambridge; and in that case, I shall have to defer my return till the 31st of May. I cannot yet tell how it will be.

The stir of this London life, somehow or other, has done me a wonderful deal of good, and I feel better than for months past. This is queer, for, if I had my choice, I should leave undone almost all the things I do.

I have bought a large Alpaca umbrella, costing 271 nine shillings. Probably I shall mislay it before my return.

I trust thou dost not burthen thyself with cares. Do drive about, and see Bath, and make thyself jolly with thy glass of wine.

Remembrances to Fanny, and love to great and small.

Thine,
NATH' HAWTHORNE.

TO MRS. HAWTHORNE

Pride's Crossing, Thursday, Aug. 8th, '61

Dearest wife,

This is a very ugly morning, and, I am afraid, will keep Julian and me at home. The old gentleman had planned a fishing expedition and will probably insist upon it pretty strenuously, in spite of the imminent danger of rain. He seems insatiable in his love of the sea, and regrets that we have but a day or two more to stay, as much as I rejoice of it.

Thou dost insist too strongly upon the inconveniences and discomforts of our present abode. I rather need to have the good side of our condition presented to me than the bad one—being sufficiently prompt in discovering the latter for myself; and this is true in almost all cases. I first look at matters in their darkest aspect, and having satisfied myself with that, I begin gradually to be consoled, to take into account the advantages of the case, and thus trudge on, in my heavy 273 way, but with the light brightening around me. Now, while this process is going on, methinks it would be more advisable to assist the beniger influence than to range thyself on the side of the sinister demon, and assure me that I am suffering a thousand inconveniences, of which I am beginning to be unconscious.

I doubt whether I could have been more comfortable anywhere else than here. The people of the house are very worthy souls, both of them, entirely unobtrusive, doing everything they can for us, and evidently anxious to give us the worth of our money— and kindly disposed, moreover, beyond money's worth. We live better than I care about living, and so well that Julian dreads the return to the simple fare of the Wayside. The vicinity is very beautiful—insomuch that if I had seen it sooner, I doubt whether I should have built my tower in Concord—but somewhere among these noble woods of white pine and near these rocks and beaches. In fact, were it not for the neighborhood of the railway, the site of this little black house would be an excellent one; for the wood is within half a minute's walk, and the shore may be reached in ten minutes. Well;—our sleeping accommodations are poor;—that is not to [be] denied, but leaving out that matter, we 274 have nothing to complain of—except the heat, which would have pervaded any abode, unless it were an Italian palace.

Mrs. Dana (the elder poet's wife, I believe) called here in a barouche the other day, while Julian and I were out, to see Una, whom she sup[posed] to be stopping here? She had two or three young ladies with her, and would probably have asked Una to make a visit at their villa.

Elizabeth came to see us, Tuesday afternoon, and brought some more books. I proposed that she should take advantage of our escort to Concord; but she says she cannot be ready before the first week of September.

It is time we were gone from hence; for everybody seems to have found us out, and Julian says the boys shout at him from the cliffs, crying "Mr. Hawthorne! Mr. Hawthorne!!" I don't know whether they mistake him for his father, or pay him these courteous attentions on his own account.

You may await tea for us on Saturday—unless the old people chance to be very hungry.

With utmost love,
N. H.

TO MRS. HAWTHORNE

(Letter 50—written by Julian Hawthorne, and continued by N. H.; no date or superscription.)

Willy has been making a topmast for his ship, but by the way I have forgot about his ship. He made it and it is 29 inches long, and about three tuns. He has made a beautiful solid balance for it and he says it looks just like a real ship he has made or is going to make

Dearest Wife,

Julian did not finish his letter; but I suppose thou wilt be glad to receive it, such as it is. It rains again most horribly to-day; so that I have been obliged to leave him at home, where he finds society enough and the greatest kindness. I believe I told you, in one of my former letters, that he has quite left off hunching his shoulders. He has complained of the headache, now and then, but not often; and Dr. Dryasdust has promised 276 to take him in hand, and entirely refit him—that is, if he prove to be out of repair.

Do not forget to tell me whether Mr. Westen's coal-bill was paid.

I hoped to have received letters from thee by the Cintra, which arrived here day before yesterday, having left Lisbon on the 15th. She reports the Madrid as having arrived on the Friday after sailing. I long to know whether thy cough yet begins to be benefitted by the sunshine, and whether thou findest again the elasticity of frame and spirit, which thou leftest behind in America. Since thou hast departed, I sometimes feel a strange yearning for the Wayside, and wish that our wanderings were over, and all of us happy together in that wretched old house.

THINE OWN OWNEST.

TO MRS. HAWTHORNE

Continental Hotel,
Philadelphia, March 9th, '62

Dearest Wife,

Wishing to spend a little while in New York, we did not leave there till 2 o'clock, yesterday, and so are not yet in Washington. I had a pleasant time in New York, and went on Friday evening, by invitation, to the Century Club, where I met various artists and literary people. The next forenoon, Ticknor strolled round among his acquaintances, taking me with him. Nothing remarkable happened, save that my poor old bedevilled phizmahogany was seized upon and photographed for a stereoscope; and as far as I could judge from the negative, it threatens to be fearfully like.

The weather here is very warm and pleasant; there are no traces of snow and it seems like the latter end of April. I feel perfectly well, and have a great appetite. The farther we go, the deeper grows the rumble and grumble of the coming 278 storm, and I think the two armies are only waiting our arrival to begin.

We expect to leave Philadelphia at 8¼ tomorrow morning, and shall reach Washington at 6 o'clock P.M. It I have an opportunity, I shall send off Una's note the same evening, but cannot tell how. 279

TO MRS. HAWTHORNE

Dearest Wife,

I have been particularly well yesterday and to-day. You must particularly thank Mr. Fields for the two volumes of the magazine. The article about Lichfield and Uttoxeter is done; and I shall set about the remaining article for the magazine in a day or two, and probably get it finished by the end of the month, since it will not be necessary to hurry. I shall call it "Civic Banquets," and I suppose it will be the concluding article of the volume.

I want a new hat, my present one being too shabby to wear anywhere but at home; and as Mr. Fields is all made up of kindness, I thought he might be kind enough to get me one at his hatter's. I have measured my old hat round outside of the hatband, and it is about 24 inches; inside, it measures 7 inches one way, and a little more than 8 the other, and is hardly large enough. 280 Get the largest hat possible; color black, a broad brimmed slouch.

Thank Rose for her kind letter.

(On the reverse side of the foregoing letter appears the following, written by Una)

All Rose's side of the hawthorn is covered with buds, and my wild violets are rampant. I water your hawthorn branches every morning, and as yet they have showed no signs of fading, though Papa, with his usual hopefulness, declares they will. We found today on the hill a lonely violet, the first of that sisterhood.

Julian appears well and jolly, but yesterday we were all killed by eating newly-dug horse-radish, which was as pungent as a constellation of stars. Papa stamped and kicked, and melted into tears, and said he enjoyed it intensely, and I bore equal tortures more quietly; the impregnable Julian being entirely unaffected by it, laughed immoderately at us both.

Papa wants me to leave a place for him, so good-bye.

Your loving daughter,
UNA HAWTHORNE.

TO MRS. HAWTHORNE

Dearest wife.

I have nothing to say except that a hen has vouchsafed to lay two eggs in our barn, and I have directed that one shall be left as a nest egg; so that you can have a fresh dropt egg every morning for breakfast, after your return.

Una has considerably improved our table; and I like this new cook much better than poor Ann.

Do not mind what Una says about staying away longer, but come whenever you like; though I think you have hardly been away long enough to want to see us again.

TO MRS. HAWTHORNE

Boston, July 3d, 3½ o'clock

Dearest Wife,

Mr. Fields tells me that a proof sheet was sent to Concord to-day, and he wishes it to be sent to him in Boston, so that I may look over it on Monday. You must put two one-cent postage stamps.

This has been a terrifically hot day. I shall leave for Concord (N. H.) at five o'clock, and shall mail this scribble there, so that you may know that I have arrived safely.

> With love to the old people,
> Thine,
> N. H.

TO MRS. HAWTHORNE

The Wayside, Sunday morng., Sept. 29th

Dearest,

We were disappointed in not receiving a letter last night, but doubt not all is going on well with you;—only that miserable headache. Why was this world created? And thy throat too—which thou wilt never be at the trouble of curing.

We get on bravely here, in great quiet and harmony; and except that life is suspended (with me, at least) till thou comest back again, I do not see how things could go better. We tried hard to be wretched on Fast Day, in compliance with thy advice; but I think it did not succeed very well with the two young people; nor could I perceive that anybody really fasted, except myself, who dined on potatoes and squash, as usual. I did purpose indulging myself in a plate of hot soup; but thy exhortations were so earnest that I gave up the idea, and am doubtless the better for my 284 abstinence—though I do not as yet see that the country has profited thereby.

Mr. Wetherbie came to see me with his bill; but I informed him of thy orders not to pay it without some subtraction, and told him he must await thy return—which he seemed not unwilling to do. He is going to the wars!—as a dragoon!!—for he says he has all his life been fond of military service, and the captain of his troop is an "old military associate." Thou wouldst have thought, to hear him talk, that this gallant Wetherbie was a veteran of at least twenty campaigns; but I believe the real motive of his valiant impulses consists in his having nothing else to do, and in his being dazzled by the sight of $200 in gold, which W. brought home—where he could have got it (unless by robbing the dead) I can't imagine; for his wages for three months would not have been more than $40. But really, dearest, the spirit of the people must be flagging terribly, when a sick old man like Wetherbie is accepted as a bold dragoon! It shows that good soldiers cannot be had.

Julian has had his hair cut according to his own notions; so thou must expect to see a scarecrow.

Do not thou come home on Wednesday, if it can do any good either to thyself or Bab to stay 285 longer. But thou hast still another expedition to make, and the cold weather will soon be upon us. Kiss Bab for me and believe me

THY OWN OWNEST.

9 781835 526071